VENUS ON THE FAIRWAY

*Creating a Swing—and a
Game—That Works
for Women*

Debbie Steinbach

with Kathlene Bissell

Foreword by Hollis Stacy,
three-time U.S. Women's Open Champion

Contemporary Books

Chicago   New York · San Francisco   Lisbon   London   Madrid   Mexico City
Milan   New Delhi   San Juan   Seoul   Singapore   Sydney   Toronto

Library of Congress Cataloging-in-Publication Data

Steinbach, Debbie.
   Venus on the fairway : creating a swing—and a game—that works for women /
Debbie Steinbach with Kathlene Bissell ; foreword by Hollis Stacy.
      p.   cm.
   Includes index.
   ISBN 0-8092-9982-8
   1. Golf for women.   I. Bissell, Kathlene.   II. Title.
GV966.S74   2001
796.352'3'082—dc21   00-48611

Contemporary Books
A Division of The McGraw·Hill Companies

1 2 3 4 5 6 7 8 9 0   VL/VL   0 9 8 7 6 5 4 3 2 1

ISBN 0-8092-9982-8

This book was set in Sabon
Printed and bound by Vicks Lithograph

Cover design by Nick Panos
Cover and interior photographs by Warren Keating

McGraw-Hill books are available at special quantity discounts to use as premiums and
sales promotions, or for use in corporate training programs. For more information, please
write to the Director of Special Sales, Professional Publishing, McGraw-Hill, Two Penn
Plaza, New York, NY 10121-2298. Or contact your local bookstore.

This book is printed on acid-free paper.

"I think, therefore I am."
RENÉ DESCARTES—PHILOSOPHER, MALE

"I feel, therefore I am."
DEBBIE STEINBACH—PROFESSIONAL GOLFER, FEMALE

CONTENTS

FOREWORD

Debbie (Meisterlin) Steinbach and I met in the summer of 1970. I was the hotshot from Georgia, and she was the hotshot from California—both of us competing in the Broadmoor Invitational, a national tournament with players from all over the world.

Now we are both in our forties, having survived many a crisis, and here I am writing the foreword to her book, which will revolutionize the teaching of golf to women. *Venus on the Fairway* contains a refreshing approach to teaching women the game I love, and will most assuredly change the way both men and women look at golf.

This book is full of serious information. Debbie's humor will not disguise her knowledge of the game—but try not to laugh too much, or you will miss out. She is not just funny, but also brilliant in the way she explains the complexities of golf through humor.

We live near each other in La Quinta, California, so we often have the opportunity to visit. Because we also belong to the same golf course in La Quinta, The Palms, we play and get together on the driving range whenever time allows.

When Debbie was first debating whether to write this book, I asked her what was the book's premise. As she explained the differences between men and women in golf, particularly the hip turn, I understood exactly what she was saying.

I went back to hitting golf balls and started focusing on my own hip turn. Almost instantly I gained back the 20 yards I had been missing for a long time! This is how my best swing feels—I just wasn't aware of how my hip turn affected this feel.

I told Debbie she had to write the book! I also promised her I would write the foreword. I am not sure she thought I would actually come through, but I would not have it any other way. I am thrilled to be a part of this, and why not? I salute you, Debbie—and I am proud of you, my dear friend. You did it!

Hollis Stacy

ACKNOWLEDGMENTS

Like most things I enjoy doing in my life, this book has been very much a "team" effort. First, thank you, to my husband, John, for loving me and encouraging me to accomplish all that I can.

To Kathy Bissell, thank you for believing in my vision and helping to bring it to completion. Your writing experience and organizational skills were invaluable. Many thanks to Rob Taylor and Contemporary Books for signing on early, which gave me the confidence I needed to throw myself into this 100 percent. Without a deadline, it would have taken me ten years! And also to Kathy Dennis, my project editor, who worked overtime to keep me focused.

Thank you to my panel of doctors: Dr. Maxann Shwartz, for being the one and only "Dr. Max." You are a wonderful golf instructor and psychologist, but you are even a better friend. Dr. Frank Crinella, for sharing so much of your knowledge and research. More important, thank you for helping me to find "my" swing! Dr. Bruce Ogilvie, for taking time out of your busy schedule to meet with me and share your interesting research. You are a wonderful human being, I thank you also for your genuine concern for and support of women. Dr. Rome Hanning, for supporting me by reading through various chapters to check for any errors or omissions. You have always been there for me from when I was a child and I will always love you for that. Dr. Bob Spaan (The Wiz), thank you for all of the crazy lunches we spent together while you encouraged and challenged me to come up with new ideas. I love working with you because although you may be brilliant, you are also so much fun!

To Brett Stewart, thank you for being the male golf model on a hot summer day, when we both knew you were supposed to be at home taking care of the kids! To Warren Keating and his wife, Lisa, the only photography team I would consider for this book. Warren is a true artist, and Lisa brings out the best in him. Thank you also to Van McDaniel for supporting me by showing up on a 115-degree day to take pick-up shots with his trusty camera just in case I needed some backups. They came out great! Another big thanks to my friend and makeup artist Cynthia Zane for working her magic for the cover photo.

A big thank-you to all of my many proofreaders and supportive friends, starting with Marcia Hoyt (if this material got past Marcia, I knew it was a winner!). Also Marcy Smothers, Terry Cronin, Charlotte Grone, Wadie McDaniel, Pat Norton, Jennie Robinson, Andy Brumer, Cheryl Dixon, Joyce Loiseau, Diane Williams, Judy Furst, Carol Hogan, Mary Lawrence, and finally my loyal sister Claudia Tynan. You all deserve a drink on me!

A special thank-you goes to my mentor, Susan Pappas, who not only let me use her as an example in the book, but also kept me focused on my goals as I wrote. As always, Susan, you are the best! Also an Emmy-worthy thanks to my celebrity diva, Marj Dusey, who has become a great friend due to her quick wit and fun-loving personality. Marge, you can play in my foursome anytime! I could never leave out Hollis Stacy, who is not only a long-time friend, but will always be remembered as one of the finest players to have competed on the LPGA Tour. I am honored that you were able to be a part of this book. Also, a sincere thank-you to my good friend and fellow touring professional Penny Pulz, for your contribution to the video chapter. I am proud of what you have accomplished with your life since our touring days.

A proud hug goes to Kelly McDaniel for reminding me how much fun it is to learn when you have a clear and open mind. After a lesson with Kelly, I was never sure who the teacher was. A special pat on the back goes to Nancy Saunders for being my role model of courage and strength. I am proud to call you my friend and I look forward to the day that you are applauded for your actions on behalf of all women. To Chuck Hogan, thank you for giving me the permission to be me. You have made a remarkable contribution to the enjoyment of golf for young and old alike. I wish you continued success with your message and the best of times with your loving family.

I would like to express my gratitude to the LPGA Tour division for providing me the opportunity to live my dream as a player. I would also like to thank the LPGA Teaching division for giving me a new dream once my competitive days were over.

To my friends and members of The Reserve in Indian Wells, California, thank you for allowing me to work in an environment where I can hardly wait to get there! And to all of my students past and present, thank you for having been a part of my life. It is because of all of you that this book exists today. Hopefully, together, we will make a difference in how women's golf is taught from here on out. That is my dream.

Debbie Steinbach

INTRODUCTION

Golf has been a male-dominated game since its beginnings. As a result, all who have learned it have been influenced by what I call the *Y factor* ("Y" referring to the male chromosome). Don't get me wrong: I love men. I happen to be married to a great one. But when it comes to golf, it just doesn't work to teach women and men the same way.

Looking back at my own career, I can see how much I was influenced by the Y factor. My father, the almighty Y, introduced me to the game as a young child. My first golfing idol was Arnold Palmer, definitely a strong Y. My first influential instructor was the legendary Johnny Revolta, and he was followed by other well-known men like Jack Grout, Paul Runyon, Roger Ginsberg, Hank Haney, Jim Delich, Ed Oldfield, Tommy Jacobs, and Ernie Vossler.

For eleven years, I was fortunate enough to earn my living as an LPGA (Ladies Professional Golf Association) Tour professional. One of the highlights of my career was being paired with Jay Haas at the JCPenney Classic in Florida. That week, as I watched many of the top players in the world hitting on the driving range, I noticed the differences between the men's and women's swings. I was mesmerized while comparing the various swing styles. For example, Jay Haas has a wonderful golf swing, but his was not a swing I could relate to. No doubt, he could not relate to mine either!

This vision stayed with me and inspired me to ask many questions long after my Tour days were over. After retiring from competition in 1986, I became an LPGA instructor; it was time to ask the million-dollar question: "Why are women taught to play golf the same way as men?" No one had an answer.

Throughout my career on the LPGA Tour, we didn't have The Golf Channel. There were no women's golf magazines, and there was very little television exposure of women's golf other than the major championships. Few women players were aware of the well-qualified women teaching pros, such as Shirley Spork, Peggy Kirk Bell, or the late DeDe Owens.

I cannot explain or understand why I never considered taking lessons from a woman, other than to plead pure ignorance. Had I known then what I know now about the differences in teaching and communication styles between men and women, I would undoubtedly have added a few women to my impressive list of mentors.

When I moved on from the LPGA Tour and went into teaching, I continued to gain some surprising insights into the way people learn to play golf. Some of my knowledge came from firsthand experience teaching men and women separately, but the most telling information came from working at top golf schools with both men and women attending. I was shocked that the women were not achieving the same kind of success as the men, and they definitely were not having much fun.

In these schools, the instruction usually began with videotaping the students' golf swings. As you might guess, the next step was for instructors and students to review the videotapes for "problem areas" of the swing, with instructors marking the swing flaws on a monitor with a red or black pen. After this diagnosis, students went back out to the range with instructors to begin the process of "fixing" the swing.

The men loved this game plan, and they actually bonded with each other as they proceeded to the driving range to do some serious "problem solving." The range became something of an operating room for the guys as they performed surgery on their golf swings. Considering the way the male brain is wired, this is an ideal learning situation. They love it, and it works for them.

Unfortunately, this approach doesn't work so well for women. A woman's brain is not wired the way a man's is, and most women aren't attracted by the challenge of "fixing things." In fact, women in these schools were downright demoralized upon learning that they were doing just about everything wrong. Most were depressed after the initial video presentation.

Women don't particularly like to watch themselves on videotape, partly because appearance is a major issue with many of them. Half the women I worked with never got beyond how they looked on camera. Most were concerned about their weight, hairstyle, or funny golf outfit. The swing was secondary.

As it turns out, one problem is that women internalize negative feedback. Requiring women to watch themselves on video for the stated purpose of "fixing" themselves was about the worst way to start a learning experience. With this approach, the female students looked more like they were on life support than on the road to recovery!

I knew there had to be a better way.

Over the years, I started questioning fellow teaching pros about the way they taught women to play golf versus the way they taught men. The feedback was unanimous: there were definite differences between men and women golfers beyond the obvious. Differences in body and mind. Differences that might call for a new method.

Finally, in 1997 I had a chance to turn my developing idea into a reality. I was involved with three-time U.S. Women's Open champion Hollis Stacy and Dr. Maxann Shwartz, psychologist and LPGA professional, in developing a new program called The Disney Golf School for Women in Orlando, Florida. All three of us agreed to create a new blueprint for female students. This was our opportunity to make a difference.

Dr. Max and I interviewed the well-respected Dr. Bruce Ogilvie, who serves on the Women's Sports Foundation. Since the 1960s, he has worked with some of the greatest female athletes of all time and has done extensive research on both men and women in sports. He has been involved with many Olympic teams.

According to Dr. Ogilvie, there are significant physical and psychological differences between the sexes that affect training and performance for all sports. In fact, Olympic coaches commonly train men and women athletes using separate methods. In our interview, Dr. Ogilvie expressed amazement that golf was so far behind other sports in developing different approaches for men and women.

Dr. Max and I knew we were on to something. We shared our information with Hollis, and together we came up with a creative teaching plan for our school. In summary, we decided on the following plan.

- Rather than trying to "fix" our students, we would focus only on creating a swing that worked for each woman individually.
- By practicing several drills to enhance the "feeling" of the new swing motions, we would give women a way to experience their swings rather than an overload of knowledge.
- By adopting a positive teaching mode, we would ensure that women would have fun while learning—and thus learn better.

When we completed the golf school, it was no surprise to us that our new teaching method had been overwhelmingly successful. The women had improved their games, and we had kept it simple. Hollis, Dr. Max, and I toasted each other well into the night.

In the summer of 1999 the vision of a new teaching method for women was revived when I was paired for 18 holes with Dr. Frank Crinella of the University of California–Irvine. Dr. Crinella is a very good player himself—but, more important, he has been researching the physiology of golf swings for the last twenty years. He has worked extensively with both PGA (Professional Golfers' Association) and LPGA pros, documenting and developing computerized models of golf swings.

Dr. Crinella confirmed through his extensive research that men and women cannot swing the same way and get good results. There are several reasons, such as differences in strength, body shape, hip flexibility, muscle mass, hormones, and center of gravity. The bottom line is, women do need a different method, a different pattern—what golf pros would call a different swing model.

His research proved that my theory was right. Now I had science on my side! Dr. Crinella and I began meeting on a regular basis so I could understand more about the differences in male and female physiology and so we could play golf and test new theories, using me as the guinea pig.

The results:

- I gained 20 yards off the tee.
- My ball flight is higher.
- I am hitting the ball with the prefered right to left curve through the air.
- Dr. Crinella wants me to go back on the Tour. (I don't think so!)

Up until now, golf instruction has not been separated into sexes, except on the tees. While I have seen many progressive changes in women's golf, this is the most exciting breakthrough I have experienced. Now that we have entered the twenty-first century, the timing could not be better to raise the level of awareness of the need for improved methods of golf instruction for women.

My goal is to open your mind to the possibility of change and for you to create your very own personalized golf swing. Finally, you will no longer have to be concerned with any X, Y, or Z factor. It will be yours, as in Y-O-U!

PART I

THE Y FACTOR
FUNDAMENTALS

NEWS FLASH! WOMEN AND MEN ARE DIFFERENT

Marcy Smothers and I are the best of friends. Marcy is married to comedian Tommy Smothers, and she has two small children who keep her more than busy. Golf is an important outlet and social event that helps Marcy maintain her sanity.

I, on the other hand, work full time as a golf instructor during the day and come home to one very large child. He weighs more than 200 pounds, and his name is John. He is, of course, my husband.

Whenever our calendars allow, Marcy and I make time to get together to play the game we love and catch up on each other's lives. This means we often tee it up with our husbands. The first order of things is to put our bags on the same cart so we can go do our thing, and the guys can do theirs. If you could hear the conversations in the guys' cart and Marcy's and mine, you would understand why this book had to be written.

It is as though we are playing two separate games. Tommy loves to concentrate on his swing mechanics, always taking extra practice swings to check his positions and swing plane. Of course, John eggs him on by putting in his two cents regarding Tommy's swing and even commenting on the equipment Tommy is using.

Eventually, they both pull out their newest toys and proceed to compare the equipment, so to speak. They seem to be in a problem-solving world that Marcy and I know nothing about, and we don't care to go there!

Although our games are important, the atmosphere is more social. Marcy and I talk about family, friends, and the latest Oprah show. We are not interested in all the technical blather of the game. We just want to play, relax, and enjoy each other's company. Every time we look over at the guys, they are either tossing up grass to check the wind or pulling out their yardage binoculars to get the exact distance to the hole. It is obvious they are having a wonderful time sharing their passion for the game, but to Marcy and me, they might as well be rocket scientists!

Taking a Closer Look

I know intuitively that when it comes to golf, women and men are very different. However, I also know that every individual—male or female—is unique. So even though I speak in general terms of traits characteristic of men and women, I understand that there are exceptions to all of these "rules." That said, let us look deeper into this phenomena.

Before I started playing couples golf with my husband, I had suspected that there were differences between men and women when it comes to playing and learning golf. Some of them are so obvious that you would have to be an alien to miss them.

John Gray, Ph.D., has made a fortune writing books—the best known being *Men Are from Mars, Women Are from Venus*, which explores the many differences between men and women in attitudes and communication styles. His success and popularity have been mind-boggling. In fact, this subject matter has become such a hot topic, I cannot help but ask, "Why has no one brought this concept to the game of golf?"

Men and women approach things differently. One way is no better than the other—just different. My good friend Dr. Maxann Shwartz uses the example of changing the oil in your car to explain how differently women and men think. She will ask a group of men and women, "How many of you know how to change the oil in your car?" We see the majority of the men raise their hands, yet we rarely see any of the women raise theirs. The next question is, "How many of you want to know how?" The women still don't raise their hands. The truth is, women couldn't care less about changing oil—they just want to drive the car!

Golf is much the same way. Spare us the details and technical minutia. *Keep it simple—we just want to play golf.* Golf is a recreational experience for women. It doesn't have to be brain surgery.

Dr. Bruce Ogilvie, a world-renowned physiologist who has studied the different ways men and women Olympic athletes train, has found that women are less inclined to desire cognitive feedback than men—which is a fancy way of saying that women don't want as much factual or theoretical information. He also confirmed that women internalize negative feedback more than men do. I see this borne out every day. My female students will say, "Don't tell me what is wrong, just tell me what you want me to do." With a female student, I play the role of a trusted teacher. I keep it short, simple, and positive.

5

A male student, on the other hand, will likely start a lesson by telling me everything he knows he is doing wrong, then detail his various ideas about how we should solve his problems. With a male student, I am more of a coach than with a female student, and we work together as a team to solve all the problems. Negatives are not a bad thing for a man—they are merely obstacles to be conquered.

Dr. Max explains that while women rely on their intuition to process information, men analyze by breaking things down into parts.

Mentally, men are information hounds. They are constantly asking "why" when it comes to the mechanics of golf. They believe that the more information and knowledge they gather, the better their performance will be. Men love fixing, adjusting, and tinkering. They like to take things apart, and their golf swings are no exception. Rarely have I met a man who didn't own a toolbox!

In *Men Are from Mars, Women Are from Venus*, John Gray wrote: "Men value power, competency, efficiency and achievement. They are constantly doing things to prove themselves while developing their power and skills. Their sense of self is defined through the ability to achieve results. They experience fulfillment primarily through success and accomplishment." What better immediate feedback to validate oneself than to hit a golf ball 300 yards!

Dr. Gray added: "Women value love, communication, beauty and relationships. They spend a lot of time supporting, helping, and nurturing one another. A woman's sense of self is defined through her feelings and the quality of her relationships. They experience fulfillment through sharing and relating."

This certainly explains why women derive such a sense of satisfaction from playing golf with friends and family. It also explains the boom in couples golf.

This is not to imply that women do not enjoy or are not motivated to play great golf—they are. I would not have competed on the LPGA Tour for eleven years if I did not want to play great golf. Everybody, men and women alike, enjoys doing something well. I will say, though, that I probably enjoyed the pro-ams a lot more than players on the PGA Tour did. The pro-ams were right up my alley—social and fun!

Physical Differences

One of my first research goals for this book was to meet with Dr. Frank Crinella. I had heard about his research with top male and female golfers, and I wanted to know whether he had discovered any significant differences between the two when it came to the golf swing. At that first meeting in his office, he stood up, walked to a blackboard, and drew a Y. He said that shape represented a male. Then he drew an upside-down Y and said that shape represented a female. I wasn't overly excited to be an upside-down Y, but I understood where he was going and I liked it.

That was the major difference in a nutshell. Anatomically, a man's shoulders are wider than his hips, and the average male torso is longer than a woman's. He is shaped like a Y. Men are generally taller, larger, and stronger than women. As they swing, they generate more power from their upper bodies because they have larger torsos, greater muscle mass and density, and bigger fingers, hands, wrists, and forearms than women.

7

Brett's shoulders are wider than his hips, while my hips are wider than my shoulders. His torso is a lot longer than mine. He's shaped like a Y, and I'm shaped more like an upside-down Y.

A woman's hips are wider and more flexible than a man's, which makes all the difference in the world when it comes to how we should swing a golf club. With so much more weight in our lower bodies, our center of gravity is lower. That influences the way we swing.

Because women are inherently more flexible, they are able to derive power through rotation and torque rather than the brute over-all strength used by most men. This extra turning action and torque created with the hips is a major difference between men and women's golf swings, according to Dr. Crinella.

Men coil their upper bodies against their back hip during the backswing, creating extra torque. This has often been called the *X factor*. Women create a similar kind of torque by turning the entire torso, including the hips, against the inside portion of the rear foot to create power.

Brett coils his shoulders into his right hip, while I coil my entire torso against the inside of my right foot and knee.

When golf instructors begin to understand that the hip area is the main power source for women golfers, instruction may never be the same again. Teaching professionals will be forced to consider different body types, rather than teaching everybody from a single swing model. Finally, women will get the attention and consideration they deserve.

Christiane Northrup, M.D., in her book *Women's Bodies, Women's Wisdom*, states that as women, "we must use our creativity, our womb power to regenerate our planet." I believe that we as women must use our "womb power" to hit golf balls. We can save the planet later!

2

THE GRIP: GETTING
A HANDLE ON
YOUR GAME

The grip is your connection to the golf club. Its purpose is to attach your hands to the club so that you can feel and control what the shaft and the clubhead are doing. I cannot emphasize enough how important it is for a woman to have the proper hold on the club if she is going to maximize her potential for extra distance. Although there is no such thing as a perfect grip, there are choices to make based on your own goals as a golfer.

I encourage distance for the majority of my female students. Giving up a little accuracy is worth adding 20 yards to their drives and 10 yards to their irons. This would make a dramatic improvement, and it all starts with how you hold the club.

There are three basic grips:

- The ten-finger, or baseball, grip
- The overlapping grip
- The interlocking grip

For beginners, I recommend the *ten-finger grip*, which is also called the *baseball grip*. As you might imagine, with this grip you hold the golf club in much the same manner as you would hold a

In the *ten-finger grip* (also called the *baseball grip*), all of my fingers are on the shaft; I hold the club in much the same way as a baseball player holds a bat. This is a great grip for beginners.

The *overlapping grip* is the most popular with Tour players.

The *interlocking grip* is famous because Jack Nicklaus uses it.

baseball bat. This is the most comfortable of the three grips, and because every finger is on the club, it is also the strongest grip of the three. Novices find it much easier to control the golf club with a baseball grip, and many of my students like it so much they never change.

After the hands gain strength and learn to work together, and the student gains confidence with her swing, I suggest changing to the *overlapping grip* (also called the *Vardon grip* after Harry Vardon) for added power. This grip is similar to the baseball grip, but the right pinky finger (for a right-handed player) rests snugly on top of the left hand between the first and second fingers.

I have rarely seen an accomplished female golfer using an *interlocking grip*, and I have not suggested it to any of my female students. It may be a good way to hold the club for Jack Nicklaus, but

I don't recommend it for women. It requires greater hand strength than most women have, and it's downright painful for golfers who have arthritis in their hands. That said, I am open to it—so if it feels good to you, go ahead and use it. The style of grip you choose is not as important as the placement or position of your hands on the club.

Understanding Terminology

Let me preface my instructions by introducing you to a little basic terminology. Because a golfer stands sideways to the target when hitting a golf ball, one side of the body is closer to the target (the hole) than the other. Therefore, when referring to aspects of the golf swing, we speak of a golfer as having a *target side* and a *rear side*. So if you are right-handed, your left side is the target side and your right side is the rear side. In the same way, if you are left-handed, your right side is the target side and your left side is the rear side. So when I speak of, for example, your rear foot, I'm referring to your left foot if you're a lefty, or right foot if you're a righty. When I refer to your target hand, I mean your right hand if you're a lefty, or left hand if you're a righty.

13

To create the power you have always wanted in your golf game, it's essential to have a sound grip. Start by placing the handle of the club in your target hand where your palm and fingers meet. Avoid placing the handle too much in the palm area. Wrap your fingers around the club until the crease between your thumb and forefinger points to your rear shoulder. You should be able to see one or two knuckles of your target hand when you look down at it. If you see your ring finger knuckle, you are seeing too many knuckles—turn your hand back under until you see only two. You should feel as though the control of the club is in the last three fingers, not the palm of your hand. Your strength and leverage is in those fingers, so use them!

Start your grip by placing the handle of the club in the crease where your palm and fingers meet on your target hand. Be careful not to let the handle rest in your palm.

Wrap your target hand around the club until you can see one or two knuckles on your target hand. You should feel as though you are gripping the club in the fingers of your target hand.

Your rear hand goes on second, and the crease made by your thumb and forefinger on the rear hand also points to the rear shoulder. Once again, you want to feel the handle of the club in the fingers of your rear hand, not your palm.

To ensure that you have the proper grip position, check to see whether the Vs created by your thumb and first finger on *both* hands point to your rear shoulder. (When you hear experts talking about where the "V" in the grip is pointed, that is what they mean.)

While you're checking, watch out for two grip errors. First, if both of your thumbs point directly down the shaft with the Vs pointing directly to your chin, you have a *weak grip*. I see this all too often with women golfers. This position not only robs you of power

Place your rear hand on the handle so you feel as though you are gripping the club in the crease between your palm and fingers. Notice how the target-hand thumb fits perfectly under the muscle pad of your rear hand.

When you have the proper grip, the creases on both hands will point to your rear shoulder, and you should be able to see two knuckles on your target hand as you look down at your grip.

15

because it limits hand action, but it can also cause slicing. A slice is a weak shot that curves to the right of your target (or to the left for left-handers).

Second, if you can see more than two knuckles when you look down at your target hand, you have a *strong grip*. That's not as good as it might sound; this grip can cause as much havoc with your golf swing as a weak grip! A strong grip encourages too much hand and wrist action, which can result in a hooked shot. A hooked shot is a fast curving shot that turns to the left of your target (or to the right for left-handers). Watch for the telltale signs of a grip that is too strong: the Vs will point beyond your rear shoulder, and more than two knuckles will show on your target hand.

It is vital to understand that your target hand controls the golf club face. By gripping the club so that you can see one to two knuckles on your target hand, you can return the club face back to square at impact so that the ball will leave the club face on a straight path. If your hand is in a weak position, you are likely to push or slice the ball off course. If your grip is too strong, you will probably do the opposite—draw or hook the ball to the left (or to the right for left-handers).

Holding the golf club in this so-called "basic" grip position is not as natural, comfortable, or easy for women as it is for men. Men can usually grip the club in a two-knuckle position with the left hand quite naturally, but women tend to grip in a more neutral or weak position at first. This is because a female's hands hang open from the

When your Vs are pointing toward your chin, your grip is in a weak position.

If you can see more than two knuckles on your target hand when you look down at your grip, your grip is too strong.

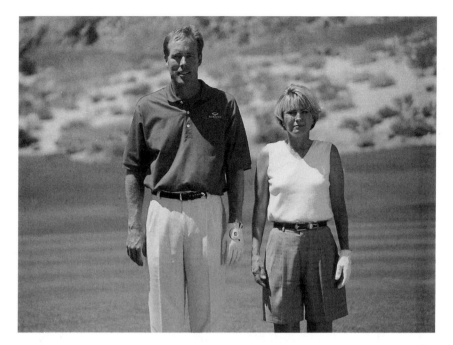

Notice how Brett's hands hang down by his side, palms pointing back.
Most men's hands will naturally hang in this closed position because of
the closed position of their elbows. A woman's hands will hang in a more
palms-open position. This is because our elbows are designed more open,
so we can achieve the "carrying angle."

elbows down. Medical experts call this phenomenon the *carrying
angle* because it enables women to easily fold their arms in a position ideally suited to carry or hold a baby.

This tidbit of information was actually a big breakthrough for me
because I struggle with this grip position myself. It may be useful that
your arms fold up if you need to carry a baby, but it's not at all helpful if you need to hold a golf club to create clubhead speed through
impact.

The bottom line is that it is not at all natural for a woman to hold
the club with the target hand in the "basic" golf grip, so women golfers need to be extra vigilant about checking for that one- or two-
knuckle position.

Now the rear (lower) hand is another story. It is much easier to place the rear hand on the grip than the target hand, and women rarely have a problem doing so. Thanks to a woman's carrying angle, the rear hand fits right under the handle and wraps around as naturally as a glove. If anything, many women get the rear hand under too far.

I first noticed this phenomenon while hitting golf balls with my husband. I joked with him that he had the arms of a gorilla! His hands were turned over so much that I could only see the backs of his hands. I was holding the club in a weaker position, while he was holding the club in a strong position with his left hand. Sure enough, I was slicing, and he was hooking—perfect cart partners!

How Hard Should I Hold On to the Club?

At address, you can start out with a relaxed grip with your target hand. But as you get to the top of your swing, you need to shift that pressure to a much firmer grip with the last three fingers of the target hand. Measuring the intensity of your target-hand grip on a scale of 1 to 10, I would say you want to be a 5–6 at address, and a 9 or 10 at the moment of transition at the top of your swing.

You are preparing to strike an object at a high speed, and it's the target hand that is controlling that club face. The last thing you need to do is to hold the club so lightly that the clubhead slips or twists when you hit the ball. Forget all this talk about holding as though you had a tube of toothpaste in your hand! If a ballplayer swung a bat like he had a tube of toothpaste in his hands, the bat would fly out every time.

Although the rear hand is the power hand, that doesn't mean you hold tighter with it. The pressure is in the thumb and forefinger and is surprisingly light. On a scale from 1 to 10, the rear-hand grip pressure is about a 5. You never want your rear hand to overpower the target hand. I have seen JoAnne Carner hit some of her best shots when her rear hand came completely off the club.

As long as you have a good, firm hold on the club with your target hand, the clubhead can strike the ball squarely at impact.

Summary

Remember, the grip is your connection to the golf club. Be sure your grip is in the fingers rather than the palms and that your Vs point to the rear shoulder. Grip pressure should be firm with the last three fingers of the target hand at the top of the swing, and lighter with the rear hand, gripping with the thumb and forefinger for control.

3

SETTING UP
FOR SUCCESS:
THE FUNDAMENTALS

I believe that at least 80 percent of golf errors occur before the club is even taken back. In this chapter, you will learn how to prevent such errors by building a strong foundation that will last a lifetime. I take these setup fundamentals very seriously. The importance of a good foundation is illustrated in the story *The Three Little Pigs*: you can build a foundation of straw, wood, or stone.

I opt for the stone foundation.

Since women generate power from "mother earth," so to speak, by using the legs and hips as the driving force for the golf swing, let's start from the ground up.

Taking a Strong Stance

The ultimate goal of the stance is to create a sturdy, balanced foundation for a coordinated, powerful golf swing. Proper placement of the feet is fundamental for building a strong stance. A woman should position her feet at least the width of her hips, measuring from the outside of the heels to the outside of the hips. This is ideal for extra power and good balance.

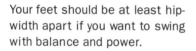

Your feet should be at least hip-width apart if you want to swing with balance and power.

I have a hip-width stance, while Brett stands with his feet shoulder-width apart. If my feet were only shoulder width, my stance would be unstable. If Brett's stance were hip width, his stance would be unstable!

It is no longer necessary for women to use the shoulders as the reference for foot position when taking a golf stance. As we already know, many women have narrower shoulders than hips. By taking a stance at least the width of the hips, a woman is set to make a stronger weight shift to her rear foot on the backswing, which translates into more power.

When many of my women students first come to a lesson, they set up at address with a stance that is shoulder width or even narrower. They are so unsteady, I can usually nudge them off-balance in any direction by merely tapping them with one finger on the shoulder. The stance is just too narrow for comfort. With the wider, hip-width stance, any woman can feel as steady as a rock.

For some of you, this stance may feel too wide at first—but you will get used to it in no time. You will feel the extra stability and balance instantly. By the time you get to your longer irons, or fairway woods and driver, you may even want to go wider. Study pictures of your favorite LPGA players if you need assurance.

Many teachers are leery of a wide stance for women because they believe a wider stance inhibits the turn of the hips. Don't worry—few women have a problem turning their hips. Women's hips are built to expand and be flexible so we can bear children. If you really want to test the flexibility of your hips and have some fun with it, host a hula hoop contest with your friends and see how many men can keep that hoop going. It is hard for a man to turn his hips as freely as a woman, as you will see!

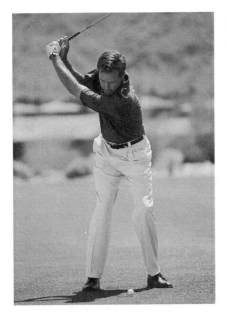

Brett swings with a large shoulder turn and little hip turn. His hips are less flexible than a woman's and his power comes from his upper body.

I swing with a larger hip turn than a man because the coil is what generates power in my swing.

Women can and should take advantage of this extra flexibility. Women generate power in the swing by turning the hips and coiling them against the knees and feet. As they uncoil and spin, they create tremendous centrifugal force, allowing for powerful impact when the clubhead meets the ball. Show me a long hitter on the LPGA Tour, and I will show you some fast-turning hips!

The Root of the Matter: Foot Position

The position of the feet is critical to a good hip turn. I suggest that women point both feet out approximately 15 degrees. This position will assist you in making a full hip turn by giving you the flexibility to move your hips freely.

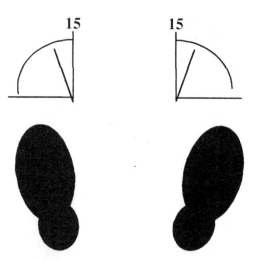

The typical stance for men is slightly different. The target foot is pointed out at a greater angle than a woman's, about 20 degrees; and the rear foot is straighter, pointed out only 5 to 10 degrees, which helps them resist the hip turn on the backswing. The extra resistance also helps them make a bigger turn with the upper body—and the bigger this turn, the more power men can generate. This extra turn with the torso against the rear hip is sometimes referred to as the *X-factor*.

This is not a relevant model for women because we are not as strong in the upper body. We do not want to restrict our hip turn as much on the backswing. Hip coil is a key power source for women golfers, so forget about restricting the hips and let them turn.

Be Flexible: The Knees Are Key

Set up to the ball with your knees bent slightly forward. Your feet cannot do their job if your knees are not flexed to provide the power to turn, push, and drive.

When I say flexed, I mean flexed forward, over your feet—not inward, facing each other. Far too many women golfers set up in this weak position, with their knees angled in toward each other (knock-kneed). I have been guilty of this myself!

25

This is a typical women's golf stance of the past. If you were taught to squeeze a beach ball between your knees for correct leg action, you can throw that visual away!

As I researched golf instruction with Dr. Crinella, I realized my own misunderstanding about how the knees work. I was taught early on to bend my knees slightly inward, as though I were squeezing a small beach ball between my knees at address. Other women golfers I know were taught to put golf balls under the outer heels of their golf shoes to achieve this same position.

But this stance actually puts undue stress on the inner portion of the knees, which is already a weak area for females. This weaker position, called the *Q angle*, occurs when women set up with their knees inside their hip line. The wider the hips, and the narrower the knees, the more severe the Q angle.

To achieve the correct knee position, bend the knees just as a tennis player setting up to return a serve. The knees should bend outward, straight forward, matching your feet.

Now my knees are in proper position, flexed over my feet.

Posture for Balance and Control

Correct posture is what gives you the stability to swing with balance, and good balance is crucial when you address the ball. All great athletes, be they dancers, jockeys, baseball players, gymnasts, or golfers, have good balance. It is vital for success in any sport.

To achieve proper posture, start with your knees bent forward over your feet. Tilt your spine forward from your hips to balance your weight over the balls of your feet. The amount of tilt you need will depend on how tall you are. You should be able to pass the "Steinbach push test": could somebody push you off-balance with two fingers? You should feel solid, as though you could catch a basketball or even a watermelon.

The forward body tilt also affects your arm position at address. A woman of average height (5′3″ to 5′6″) will have her arms and

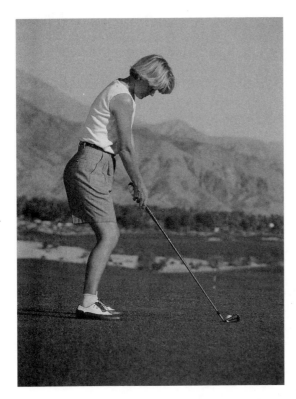

You should feel like you are totally stable at address. Ask yourself whether someone could push you off-balance with two fingers.

My hands and arms are out farther away from my body than Brett's are, approximately under my chin. Brett's are much lower, closer to his body and under his shoulders. The angle of your arms will depend on your height. Most women's arms will reach farther out because we are typically shorter than men and therefore stand more vertical at address.

hands hanging down and out on an angle, away from her body. I am 5'3" and my arms reach out at about a 45-degree angle.

Because men tend to be taller than women, they usually set up with more tilt to their upper bodies. It is not unusual for a man's arms to hang directly under his shoulders at address with no angle at all.

Good balance is what all athletes strive for. Your guide to good balance in golf is that your weight needs to be back far enough so that you can wiggle your toes, yet not be pushed over in any direction.

If you are tall and therefore have a greater forward tilt at address, you may want to let your rear end push back in order to counterbalance yourself. If you are shorter, as I am, you won't have to worry about sticking your rear end back because you will be standing in a more vertical position to start out. Have someone put you through the Steinbach push test to see just how much you need to bend at address to feel solid.

The Spine and Head

Two important leans for women in golf need to be addressed—those of the spine and head. These leans are rarely talked about in golf instruction, yet they are vital for women to create power and a higher ball flight.

Women's Power Lean #1

First, your spine will automatically lean slightly to your rear side when you grip the golf club with your target hand higher on the grip than the rear hand. Because the hands are not level, the spine is forced to lean slightly to the rear side to accommodate the lower position of the rear hand on the club.

When you grip the club correctly, your rear shoulder will naturally fall lower than your target shoulder because your rear hand is lower on the grip. This puts your shoulders into a natural tilt to the rear side.

When you take your grip, you will instantly notice that your rear shoulder is lower than the target shoulder at setup. That's good. This is the same position your shoulders will return to at impact. In time, this lean slightly behind the ball with the rear shoulder lower will actually feel natural and comfortable.

Women's Power Lean #2

Second, your head should follow your spine and lean to your rear side, so that your head is behind the ball at address rather than directly over it. Like the spine lean, the head lean should also happen automatically. It's hard to guess the degrees, but if you have power lean with your spine, the head should follow. Just be sure your head is behind the ball enough so that you are positioned where you can focus your eyes on the *back* of the golf ball, not the top of it. Envision driving a nail through the back side of the ball. Get your attention where it needs to be.

30

Because your shoulders are tilted down to your rear side, your eyes and head will be slightly behind the ball at address so that you will be looking at the back of the ball, rather than directly at the top of it. This may feel awkward at first, but this is a true power lean!

The old "keep your eyes on the ball" fundamental that we often hear does not create an athletic position at setup or impact. Actually, it may be the number-one fundamental setback for women who have learned golf in this century. Let's replace that misguided visual with a new, better instruction: keep your eyes on the *back* of the ball at address.

I suspect that this one outdated golf tip may be the reason so many women reverse pivot when they swing. By keeping the eyes directly over the ball at address, many golfers end up with shoulders that are almost parallel to the ground instead of tilting down on a natural angle (power lean #1).

It is too easy for golfers who try to focus on the middle portion of the golf ball to resist shifting weight back and then on through during the golf swing. This is because they are trying to keep their head steady over the ball. Forget that, the head moves. All good players have a certain amount of lateral movement with their heads. If you don't believe me, just watch Annika Sorenstam's head when she swings.

The Power Move

By setting up looking at the back side of the ball, you are in position to move forward on the follow-through and create some serious clubhead speed, which will get you extra distance.

The golf swing motion should feel similar to hitting a baseball, skipping a stone, or smashing a tennis forehand. These are all sidearm motions in which you step forward using your weight and momentum to create power.

Make the power lean with your spine and head at address, and you will be in the correct setup position to contact the ball with power and momentum. You can expect to hit the ball longer and higher. If your head is behind the ball at the moment of truth, you'll have a longer follow-through, more loft, and higher shots. I think you can handle that!

The "Give Me a Y" Arm Position

I am a strong believer in setting your arms in the same position at address that they will return to at impact. This means I promote what is called a slight *forward press* at address.

Rarely do I see a top woman golfer with her hands back behind or over the ball at address, with the butt of the club pointing up to the sternum. The stronger players set up with their hands slightly for-

In this weak setup position, the butt of the club is pointing at my sternum, my shoulders are fairly level, and my head is directly over the ball. I cannot possibly generate the optimum power I am capable of.

From this position, my target arm and club become one, creating a small y and allowing my rear shoulder to drop down and my head to get slightly behind the ball. Now we're talking power!

ward, with the target arm creating a straight line that runs down the club shaft and down to the clubhead. The butt of the club actually points directly under the target shoulder. Viewed from the front, your arms and club create the shape of a small "y" at address.

Although the target arm is not rigid, it is not loose either—I call this the *tree limb position*. Imagine swinging a dead tree limb—it would be stiff, and wouldn't have much whip. Now imagine swinging a live, green branch—it's limber, loose, and fast. Your target arm acts the same way in your golf swing. You don't want it to bend so much on the backswing that you lose power and control, but you don't want it to be so stiff that you lose fluidity in your swing.

The rear arm should be relaxed, especially the elbow, which should be folded enough that it points into the rear hip. Often I tease my

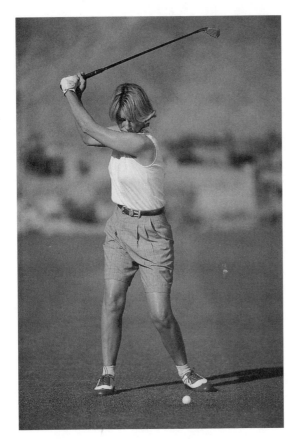

In my backswing, my target arm isn't totally stiff or straight, but bends like a tree limb. I never want a student to get so caught up in keeping that target arm straight that she stiffens up and loses the fluidity of her swing.

Rear elbow stiff: When your rear elbow is too stiff, it will cause a right-handed player's shoulders to open up to the left of the target at address. Plus, it can create tremendous tension, which will throw your entire swing plane off.

Rear elbow relaxed: My rear elbow is relaxed and ready to do its job, which is to fold during the backswing. My target arm is slightly higher than the rear arm at address, where it should be. My shoulders are set square toward the target.

students that we need to shoot some Valium into that elbow to loosen it up! Remember, the function of the rear elbow is to fold on the backswing. Relax it so it can do its job.

Relaxing that rear elbow is vital not only to greater power, but also to proper placement of your shoulders at address. A stiff rear elbow causes the upper body to be in an open position at address, and that is a major factor in causing slices.

With your arms in the proper y-position, the target arm is slightly higher at address than the rear arm due to your relaxed rear elbow and power lean. Now you are in position to use your arms effectively to sweep the clubhead away in your most natural swing plane. The arms should never be a serious problem if you simply remember to "give me a Y!"

Getting on Target: Alignment

Alignment control is an area of golf that cannot be overemphasized. You can have the best swing in the world, but if your aim is off, you are not going to be consistent. Good alignment begins with your *target line*, which is an imaginary line that extends through the ball straight to the target. The easiest way to determine your target line is to lay your golf club down where your ball should be, grip first, pointing toward your target. Eventually you will have to do this without the golf club as a guide when you play on the golf course. You can never lay down a club in competition. Instead, you'll need to rely on spot aiming behind the ball at trees in the distance, or an

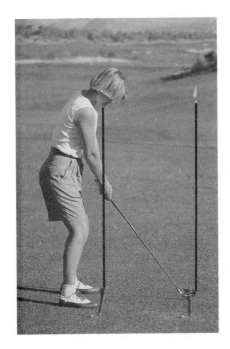

This is correct alignment. Your club face points toward the target along the target line, while your feet, hips, and shoulders are lined up on the stance line, parallel to the target line.

object a short distance in front of your ball such as weeds, leaves, sprinklers, mower marks. Pick a close spot that is in line with your target and try to hit directly over it.

To hit the ball straight, you want to swing along this target line at impact. Your club face needs to be square to the target line as well. Learning to square that club face to your target line is the magic move for consistent ball striking. Make certain that you always aim with the *bottom line* of the golf club, meaning the sole portion. Don't let that top line throw you off, because it will.

Another alignment aid is your *stance line*, which runs parallel to the target line. Think of these two lines like a railroad track—both are going the same direction and run side by side. The top rail is the

When you are set square to the target, all you have to do when you swing is use the target line as the guide for your clubhead.

target line and the bottom rail is your body line. By setting up with your shoulders, hips, and feet parallel to your target line, you are aligned in a "square" set up position with the target.

I encourage you to use this square alignment for all of your short irons, up through your 5-iron. By setting your body and feet parallel to your target line, you will be in a square alignment position to hit the ball straight. If you are looking for extra distance, you can make a slight adjustment in your stance line for your long irons and woods. Set up in a *closed position* with your feet, hips, and shoulders. It's easy to get there—just drop the rear foot

I suggest that women golfers drop the rear foot back an inch or two for extra distance, especially with the woods. This is referred to as a *closed stance.*

back an inch or two. I have found this change encourages women to swing with a more inside-to-out swing path and creates more of a draw ball flight, which means it crosses the body line. This increases the roll of the ball and adds more distance.

Ball Position

Ball position is a highly individualized fundamental. I have taken lessons from some of the greatest teachers in the world, and they all had a different philosophy regarding ball position.

I know women want more height with their golf shots because the higher you can hit the ball in the air, the easier it is to make it stop on the green or clear that bunker out on the fairway. To hit it higher, I encourage women to position the golf ball up farther in their stance than I do most men.

By moving the ball forward in the stance, women can take full advantage of the loft on the club face at impact, therefore hitting with a higher ball flight. Of course, there are always exceptions I

It is important to position the ball for your short irons and wedges farther back in your stance toward your back foot to ensure a blow that will result in a nice divot. Never feel bad about taking a divot; it's OK to hit Mother Earth, she will forgive you!

Feel free to position the ball for your mid-irons slightly closer to your target foot. This is a longer swing with a more sweeping motion, so you don't need to be concerned with taking divots. The goal is to swing on the level of the golf ball.

take into consideration—but because ball flight is so important for women if they are to stop the ball on the green, I do take ball position very seriously. The key is to find what works best for you. Experiment on your own, get comfortable with the ball flight you like for your shots, and choose for yourself.

That said, I will give you the same advice I give to my ladies group at The Reserve in Indian Wells, California. For the sand wedge through the 8-iron, position the ball midway between your feet. This lets you swing downward on a steeper angle into the ball. You should be taking a divot with these shorter irons. If you are not, particularly with your wedges, you are most likely not playing the ball back enough in your stance.

The ball position for fairway woods and the driver is anywhere from two inches inside the target heel to just off the heel itself. Notice how I play my woods just inside my target heel with my back foot dropped back slightly, creating a closed stance.

For the rest of your irons, position the ball slightly forward of center a couple of inches toward your target foot.

Finally, by the time you take your stance with a fairway wood or driver, you should be setting up with the ball at least two inches inside your target heel. I have seen many women who set up to their drivers with the ball just inside their heel, and they hit it just fine! Go watch some of your favorite LPGA pros and see where they position the ball in their stance.

The Boob Factor

Contrary to commentator Ben Wright's claim that women have trouble swinging around their breasts, this problem is not exclusive to women. I have seen plenty of men who have pecs bigger than I will ever experience in this lifetime!

Anyone, male or female, who is stocky or well-endowed on top needs to set up in a position that allows the upper body to swing freely. The key is to study the position at the moment of truth: impact.

If you study the top players at impact, you'll see that all return to impact with their target arm pushed tightly on top of and across their target-side breast area. Heavy, thin, big-busted, small-busted—they are all in the same position at impact with that target arm.

40

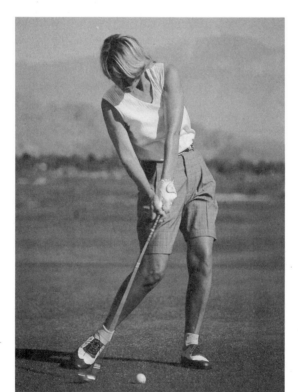

The breasts should not be a factor at all when you set up with your target arm on top of the breast on your target side and your rear elbow relaxed and pointing down to your rear hip. All you should be concerned with is returning to impact in the same position.

So the boob factor is no factor at all if you simply set up with the target arm on top of the breast on the target side at address, exactly the same position it needs to return to.

In the past, many pros would teach players to set both arms over the breasts, or both arms under them. What kind of thinking is this? Take them out of play and let your target arm turn back along with your torso.

When I give a barrel-chested man a lesson, and he sets up with his hands low and inside so he literally cannot swing his arms back across his body, I give him the identical golf tip that I tell my bigger-busted women: "Place target arm on top of the boob at address!"

A Picture Is Worth a Thousand Words

As we come to the close of the setup segment, I feel it is important to leave you with a lasting vision of a balanced and functional setup.

If you were a first-time student on my lesson tee, I would physically position you into a well-balanced, coordinated setup position. Then, while you were in your ideal setup position, I would take an instant picture of you from the front and from the side so you could take those pictures home and place them on your refrigerator. With these pictures to look at every day, you cannot help but to implant in your brain the image of what you want to achieve.

Obviously, I cannot take a picture of you, but thanks to my good friend and three-time U.S. Open champion Hollis Stacy, we have come up with the next best thing. Hollis and I were playing golf recently while she was in town training for yet another LPGA event. She graciously volunteered to be our stand-in model for the book.

Hollis has what is considered to be a "classic" setup and swing—they are textbook examples of what we have covered so far in this book. Thanks, Hollis, for allowing us to dub you "The Refrigerator Pro."

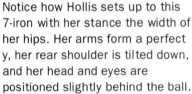

Notice how Hollis sets up to this 7-iron with her stance the width of her hips. Her arms form a perfect y, her rear shoulder is tilted down, and her head and eyes are positioned slightly behind the ball.

Hollis bends naturally at the hips and has the proper amount of flex in her knees. She is centered and balanced in an athletic position. (No wonder she plays so well on the LPGA Tour!)

If you choose, you can clip these photos and stick them on your refrigerator door so you can immediately start creating an image of a strong and functional golf setup position. When you feel your own setup is where you want it to be, your hair is done, and you are wearing your best golf outfit, simply replace Hollis with pictures of yourself. Visualization is a powerful tool. Monkey see, monkey do.

Congratulations! You've reached the end of the fundamentals section! Now it is time to move on to learning what the motion of a good swing "feels" like.

PART II

THE BASICS OF
IMPACT AND SWING

4

IMPACT:
GETTING IN
TOUCH WITH YOUR
FEELINGS

Feeling the correct impact position clears your head of all the technical spiderwebs in your brain and allows you to swing from your senses. This is the goal of your golf swing—to make contact with the ball in the center of the clubhead in a square and powerful impact position. That is why impact is often called "the moment of truth." This is that magical experience that sets off the lightbulb over your head. It says, "Yeah, this is it! I got it!"

I am a broken record when it comes to my philosophy about the golf swing: there is no wrong or right way to swing a golf club, period. The motion of most golf swings is undeniably variable. Nancy Lopez, Juli Inkster, Karrie Webb, and every other great player has her own distinct swing, yet they all look almost identical at impact.

The key is to know your goal at that moment of truth, know where you want your body and clubhead to be at impact. When you have a vivid mental image of what that position looks like and you have developed a sense of how that position feels in your muscles, you can swing with a sense of certainty, confidence, and intention you never dreamed possible.

What's even more exciting is that correct impact position is easy to learn. For many students, this is the missing link that transforms them from lost lambs into competent golfers, instantly.

It is my hope that one day, all golfers will be introduced to golf by starting at impact. No more confusion with all the ninety-nine dos and don'ts regarding the backswing! Let me demonstrate the power of understanding impact position by sharing with you a story about one of my younger little lambs, Kelly.

Kelly's Story

Kelly McDaniel is a twelve-year-old junior golfer who hopes to be an LPGA Tour player someday (that or an engineer, of course). She had been through group lessons and a couple of years of individual instruction. Tournaments are a big part of her summers, and that is why she came to see me.

Meet Kelly McDaniel. She is an enthusiastic twelve-year-old who wants to play on the LPGA Tour someday.

Kelly was frustrated with the length she was driving the golf ball, particularly with her driver. She had moved up in her age class in competition and felt she could be more competitive if she could gain 10 to 15 yards off the tee.

I started Kelly the same way I do all of my students, having her hit into an impact bag. (More on this tool later.) We could then check her position at the moment of truth. Kelly had never done anything like this before, so I had her attention. We started out using a 7-iron and immediately found out why she was hitting the ball short and to the right.

First, her clubhead was coming into the ball in an open position, so she had been pushing and sometimes slicing the ball. Second, her head was leaning forward at impact and getting in front of the ball, causing a tremendous loss of power and control.

Curing the open club face was easy—I just had Kelly exaggerate the feel of swinging the clubhead into the impact bag with the toe portion of the club striking the bag first. After about six swings, Kelly understood that what *felt* closed to her was in fact square. She could both feel and hear the difference between an open club face and a square club face at impact. Merely telling Kelly that she needed to close the face sooner would have accomplished nothing. She needed to *feel* the difference.

47

After she understood what a square club face felt like at impact, we moved on to the second issue: learning to keep her head and upper body behind the ball. This, too, would be a totally different feeling than she was used to, so I asked her if she could use her hips more rather than relying on her upper body for power.

Kelly confessed that she had been working very hard not to use her hips so much. Her previous pro had told her that she had excessive hip action. He wanted her to use them as little as possible so she could swing more with her upper body.

This is a popular teaching theory today for men. I know it works for a lot of the PGA pros. But this is not great advice for a young girl! I promptly gave Kelly permission to use as much hip action as she felt she could control. Immediately she started hitting that bag as though she were Dottie Pepper. Her hips were leading and her head stayed behind the ball at impact.

We moved up to the practice tee and put a driver into Kelly's hand. Neither of us will ever forget her first swing with that driver. The ball traveled at least 20 yards longer than any previous drive!

Kelly held her finish for what seemed like forever as she marveled at her own talent. Then she looked over at me with her big blue eyes as if to ask, "Well?" I told her the shot was awesome, then asked, "How did that feel?"

Kelly replied with newfound enthusiasm, "Natural!" Then she asked, "Was that the right answer?" Yes, Kelly; that was the right answer!

Kelly is a perfect example of a successful learning model. Her mind is not cluttered with information, and she is swinging from her senses. You, too, can learn to swing like Kelly; all you have to do is allow yourself to be a child again; enter into the world of fast instinctive learning!

Debbie's World

Having read this far into *Venus on the Fairway*, you are now a walking encyclopedia on the subject of the golf swing. (Sorry about that, but I couldn't write a book with blank pages!) But now I need you to go through a "detox" process, clearing your mind so you can be receptive to new ideas and feelings.

The reason I use children as my learning models is obvious: they are the fastest and best learners on the planet. They are free spirits, and they seem to instinctively know the best way to learn a new skill. If you don't believe me, watch a child learning a motor skill. They care little about facts, figures, or information. Rather than relying on information, kids rely on their feelings to be their guide. They learn by experimentation.

That is the atmosphere I choose to work in during instruction. I assure students when they come for a lesson they are going to have a session that is both fun and creative. I consciously set the stage to allow errors without judgment because I know this is the mind-set that assures greater learning. I do this because it works!

If you want to create the swing that works for *you*, get out of your head and get into your senses.

The first thing you notice in my learning area is a big yellow bag sitting on the ground. This is not a gimmick to take out aggressions. This is called the *impact bag*. The goal of the bag is to stop and trap your clubhead and body at impact. It is filled with old laundry and towels, so it is cushioned. You can take a good swing at it, but you never really need or want to take a full swing.

After a few warm-ups hitting into the bag to get the knack of it, my students and I look at club positions and various body positions

Welcome to my practice area. It is hard to miss my ever-popular impact bag, my number-one instruction tool for teaching the feeling of impact.

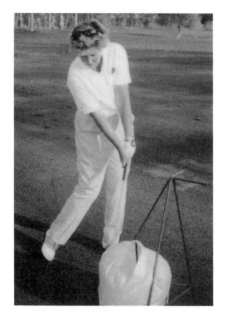

*All My
Children*

Hollis Stacy demonstrates the ideal
impact.

Georgeann before

Georgeann after

Mary Kay before

Mary Kay after

Falon before

Falon after

Carol before

Carol after

Melissa before

Melissa after

at impact. Usually first-time students hitting into the bag look and feel awkward and unbalanced when their swings are frozen at impact.

By simply repositioning them in the correct position at impact and allowing them to feel the correct position, the learning process kicks in. These are new feelings, and they feel surprisingly good!

Then, while they are in this new impact position, I take my trusty camera and snap another masterpiece for the refrigerator. This is a valuable experience; they actually feel the correct impact position, and then see what that looks like, instantly. The look of excitement on the faces of my students is priceless; many look like Kelly when she first knew she got it. They are twelve years old again.

Although a golf ball will never have the same amount of resistance or feedback as the impact bag, this new feeling of resistance can

instantly be transferred to hitting a golf ball. Immediately I move my students to the range to hit rows of golf balls so they can program this new feeling of impact into the brain. Then they go back to the bag for a few refresher swings, only to return to the range again. They are processing, and I don't want to get in the way—I just keep teeing up balls for them to hit.

We are not concerned with targets yet. Targets create judgment, and we are in the learning mode. We are searching for a feeling, not a result. The mind needs to stay clear so one can

Correct impact position

continue to process the feeling. Children never judge while they are learning. They just stay with the process.

The impact bag lesson never takes more than an hour, but when it is over the golfer's swing is changed forever. The swing corrects itself when the golfer, with a minimum of mechanical advice, simply focuses on where she wants her body to be at the moment of truth—impact.

Here are the key swing positions I look for with each student when she swings into the impact bag.

- **Grip:** Square at impact, one to two knuckles showing
- **Hands:** Forward of club head
- **Target arm:** Straight, tree limb position
- **Rear arm:** Elbow folding into side at impact
- **Hips:** Turning open toward target
- **Target leg:** Straight
- **Rear knee:** Bending in toward target knee
- **Rear foot:** Weight shifting up and on to rear toe
- **Head:** Slightly behind bag at impact

The impact bag is a wonderful way to get people in touch with their feelings. Although I strongly believe it is a tremendous learning tool for both men and women, I am the first to admit that guys are rarely as excited about it as the gals. I don't know if it is because they feel silly swinging into a yellow bag, or they don't like the sound it makes. Not surprisingly, women love the bag lesson so much, at least 50 percent of them drive directly from their lesson to buy an impact bag from the local golf equipment store. The proprietor tells me he can hardly keep them in stock, thanks to all my students!

I hope you now have an idea how important it is to feel the correct impact position. To be squarely against the ball at impact, you must do a lot of things right. But you don't have to think of those ninety-nine swing positions!

If you stick with this new learning model, feeling your swing rather than intellectualizing it, you will never lose that wonderful feeling of correct impact for longer than it takes to retune it on the impact bag. You will definitely remember the feel! Using the impact bag is like riding a bike: once you get it, you have it forever. As Kelly said, "It's natural!"

You may now resume putting information back into your mental computer, creating the swing that works for you. Be careful that as you program information back into your brain, you do so byte by byte. Your brain is like a computer—if it takes in more information than it can handle, it overloads and crashes.

If you are interested in getting an impact bag of your own, check out the ordering information at the end of the book.

5

THE FULL SWING:
PLANE AND SIMPLE

This chapter was a struggle for me. I can explain the technical aspects of the swing, and I can visually demonstrate it, but I can't really tell you how the swing should *feel*. This feeling is an experience, and no one can really know what another person is experiencing.

For example, if I were to teach you how to ride a bike, I could tell you what you need to do and show you what those steps look like. But until you got on that bike and actually felt what it is like to steer, pedal, and balance—all at the same time—you would not really learn to ride a bike. Golf is no different. It is a motor skill that is learned through experience.

As we assemble the pieces of the full swing, bit by bit, keep in mind that these are all pieces of a puzzle. When they are put together they form a complete picture: *your* golf swing.

Building the Arc: You Gotta Have Heart!

The *arc* of the swing is the circular path your clubhead makes when you swing back and through. The motion is much like a wheel spin-

The hub of your arc is your heart, because your forward press at address positions the grip of your club pointing toward your heart.

ning around your chest at an inclined angle (the *swing plane*, which we will discuss soon). The longer and wider your wheel, the faster you will swing the club; and the faster you swing the club, the farther the ball will travel.

The hub of your wheel is your heart, and your club is a spoke. In the proper address position your hands and arms are pressed forward slightly, so your target arm is in its tree limb position. The grip of your club should be pointing at your heart.

From this position, the triangle formed by your shoulders and arms needs to move as a unit with your chest. This is sometimes referred to as a *connected takeaway* because all of the body parts are moving back together, rather than independently of each other. By swinging as a unit from the natural triangle that is formed at setup, you should be able to turn from the ball on the backswing and generate the maximum arc for your size and height. Turn your shoulders away from the ball, sweeping your arms and hands back together, keeping the butt of your club pointing toward your heart in the y-position.

Swing everything back together
as a unit.

I've outlined the steps of the swing showing the proper arc in the photos on pages 60–62. It all begins with correct setup position: my target arm and club form one line, my shoulders are tilted, and my head is just behind the ball. My knees are slightly flexed, and my legs are at least hip width. The center of my arc is my heart (a).

As I take the club back, my shoulders and hips turn together as my rear elbow begins to fold in (b). My target arm remains fairly straight as my chest continues to turn (c); again, because my heart is the hub of my arc, my swing motions revolve around it.

My hips continue to turn as my weight shifts to my right (d), and my chest is still turning with my shoulders as the club moves up to the top of the swing (e). At the top of the swing, I am completely coiled. Everything has moved back together in a circle around my heart, and I am now braced against the ground to return to impact (f).

As I begin the forward swing, my hips are unwinding and my arms and hands follow. My heart is still the center of my swing (g). When the ball has been hit, my target arm is directly on top of my target-side breast (h). As my arms extend out and away from my body, my

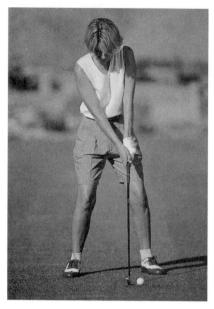

a

b

c

d

e

f

g

h

i

j

k

l

hips are completely turned open to the target (i). My right knee is turned in, causing my rear heel to come high off the ground (j). The momentum of the swing carries me around so that by follow-through, I am directly facing my target (k). I finish in a relaxed and balanced position, the natural result of a correct arc and swing (l).

Congratulations on understanding the arc. Welcome aboard!

Da Plane, Da Plane!

As teaching guru Chuck Hogan so humorously points out, the swing plane is not a small airplane dangling from your golf club. It is, unfortunately, more complicated than that! The *swing plane* is the angle your club makes when you swing your arms up and around your head and then down into the ball. If your arc is like a wheel, the swing plane is the angle at which the wheel is tilted. Ben Hogan used a pane of glass to demonstrate this concept in his book *Ben Hogan's Five Lessons: The Modern Fundamentals of Golf.* Many other people have also used this image. I like it because it is a very simple and powerful visual that shows the difference between a typical male and female golfer.

Imagine that you are swinging your arms and the shaft of your club along a smooth surface (like a pane of glass). As you pull the club back on the backswing, visualize your arms and shaft painting the surface your favorite color. This is the image to keep in mind when you think about a swing plane.

Your swing plane is determined by your height and setup position. Because women are usually shorter than men, they usually swing on a flatter plane. But a tall woman, like 5′ 10″ LPGA star Helen Alfredsson, should set up and swing on a more upright plane, while a shorter woman, like 5′ Alison Nicholas, will have a swing that is dramatically flatter.

At the beginning of the swing, my hands and arms are out farther away
from my body than Brett's are, approximately under my chin. Brett's are
much lower, closer to his body and under his shoulders. The angle of your
arms will depend on your height. Most women's arms will reach farther out
because we are typically shorter than men and therefore stand more
vertical at address.

As Brett and I start our swings into motion, you can clearly see some
differences. Brett is tall, so he has a lot of bend in his posture at address.
I am much shorter, so I stand more vertical at address than Brett. These
setup positions influence our swing planes.

Brett is starting his club away on a more vertical path from the ball, up and out from his body, while I am turning my club more on a circular path, to the inside and around my body.

At the top of our swings, my hands are much lower than Brett's. Mine are over the outside of my shoulder, while his are over the inside of his shoulders. He has what is regarded as an upright swing, while mine is considered a flat swing.

Looking at the photos on pages 64 and 65, you can see that compared to Brett's swing plane, mine is much lower. My height and upright posture at setup have predetermined my swing plane. My lower setup position, with my arms out farther from my body, produces a *flat* swing plane, in which the shoulders and arms move much as they do in a baseball swing. At the top of the swing, my hands are over the outside of my shoulder.

Brett has his hands much higher than I do—over the inside of his shoulder, and will return his clubhead to the ball in a more vertical position. This swing plane is referred to as *upright*. His shoulders and arms move in a plane that is shaped like a Ferris wheel. This is because he is bent more from the hips at setup.

With an upright plane, like Brett's, it is easier to hit the ball higher in the air because the clubhead descends on the ball more vertically, creating more backspin and thus higher trajectory.

With a flatter swing plane, like mine, golfers are more inclined to hit the ball on a lower trajectory. In addition, because the clubhead travels on a flatter arc and approaches the ball more from the side (similar to a baseball swing), the flat swing plane generates less backspin, which causes the ball to run more. Play for the ball to run more—there's no need to change your natural swing plane just because you want to hit the ball higher.

I am constantly reminding my female students that golf is a sidearm game. For many women, especially those under 5'6", the feeling of the proper swing plane is the same as skipping a stone on a lake. This is an important visual for women because we usually try to copy what we see on TV—and that is usually the upright swing plane of someone much taller, like Tiger Woods or Greg Norman, whose planes are virtually impossible for us to emulate. Swing on *your* natural plane!

Now that you understand da plane, let's move on to da backswing.

Backswing in Motion: The Steinbach Cork Theory

Swinging the clubhead away from the ball can be a confusing and complicated process for many golfers. The biggest and most obvious reason is tension. Because we start out from a complete standstill, it is not easy to get that club started back with rhythm or control.

Many students ask: "How do I start my backswing? With the target shoulder or target knee? How about the rear hip?" Let's simplify this right now and learn the Steinbach Cork Theory. Imagine you are a human wine cork. If the top portion of your body—the shoulders and chest—turns, the bottom portion—the hips—will turn. The same applies in reverse: if the bottom portion turns, the top will turn. Whether you focus on turning away with the triangle or with your back hip does not matter. You move all parts together as one.

Because the hips and shoulders work together for women, it makes no difference where you start your backswing; follow your personal preference. Whatever visual or feeling helps you start that club away with rhythm, use it!

I started out by imagining I was sweeping a broom on the grass to get the feeling of keeping the clubhead low to the ground. This has been a good visual aid for me because it promotes a longer extension away from the ball and increases the swing arc. But now I have a newer visualization. I tell my students to imagine rollers on the bottom of the clubhead. Picture yourself actually rolling the clubhead away from the ball. To get those rollers spinning, move that clubhead back low and with speed.

This image has worked magic with a lot of my students. In fact, Kelly has nicknamed her imaginary rollers "Rollerblades!" By rolling the clubhead away rather than picking it up, dragging it away, or opening the club face to the inside, you are creating the rhythm and extension essential for a good backswing. Now we are on a roll!

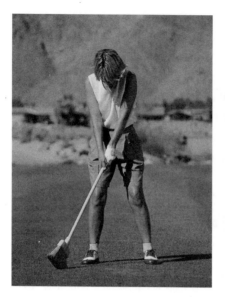 

Practicing swinging with a broom can help you keep the club low to the ground on the backswing.

Imagining rollers on the bottom of the club not only keeps the club low to the ground but adds momentum.

Swing the Y

Your arms are already in their y-position at setup. You should have no trouble maintaining this position with the backswing as you sweep or roll the clubhead away. The key is to remember that your target arm forms a straight line from your shoulder with your golf club. Your golf club is an extension of your target arm.

For your best backswing, follow these steps:

1. Move your hands and arms together. Avoid two common mistakes: Don't let your hands hinge too soon—this should happen at the top of the swing (see step 4). And don't pull your hands back away from the ball before the clubhead has started to move back. Both of these flaws will make it impossible for you

Hinging the hands too early on the backswing not only breaks the y, but negates any shoulder turn or hip turn, making it impossible to swing the shoulders, hips, and arms away in a connected motion.

Dragging the hands away on the backswing before the clubhead has started back also makes it impossible to retain the y and stay connected as one unit.

to retain the y-position and move your body parts together in the swing.

2. Sweep or roll the clubhead away from the ball. Make sure your upper body is working as a unit, and keep your y-position intact.

3. Keep your back arm relaxed so that your rear elbow will automatically fold on the backswing and be in position to support and set the club at the top of the swing.

4. At the top of your swing, your momentum forces your hands to hinge and brings your wrists into the action. It's here that your wrists fully hinge out of the y-position for a millisecond to create a powerful lever.

The rear wrist fully hinges at the top to set the club and provide optimal power, as you can see in this one-arm drill.

Ready, Set, Go

I check my students for three key positions when they get to the top of the swing:

1. **Weight shift:** The weight should fully shift to the inside portion of the rear knee and inside portion of the rear foot (but not so much that you are unstable). From this "loaded" position, you are ready to thrust forward and release leg and hip power into the downswing.

2. **Hands hinged:** The hands must be fully hinged at the top. It is not enough to create a long arc; the wrists and hands need to be involved in the swing if you are to create any distance. A stiff-wristed swing is a shortcut to short shots. Golf is a two-lever game: shoulders create the first lever, then hands become the second lever once they hinge at the top of the swing. Strong wrists and hands make a big difference for women golfers.

3. **Tray position:** The rear wrist and hand should be in such a position that they could actually hold a tray at the top of the swing. This particular visual has been around for ages, and I have

You can see from this angle that I have allowed my hips to turn fully into my rear side without shifting my weight over so much that I am sliding or swaying. I have "loaded" as much of the energy as I can muster against the inside of my rear foot, knee, and inner thigh.

never heard a better one yet. It works. From the proper set position at the top of your swing, the transition to impact will be a natural result, not a forced move.

A word of caution: be careful not to lift the right elbow and wrist up at the top of the swing. This is a common habit, but it would definitely send a tray flying to the ground! This is called a *cupped*

By letting my hands hinge at the top of my swing, I have created a wide arc with my left arm. I am using two levers for power—one with my shoulder, the other with my wrists.

Check to see if you can get that right wrist under the shaft of the club when you set your hands at the top. This tray position requires extra wrist strength.

72

position and is one of the weakest set positions a woman can swing from.

The proper forward swing is a "feeling" and thus is subject to variations for individual preferences. I feel as though I am pulling down with my upper target arm when I start the forward swing. Other players may feel as though they are leading with the target hip. Still others feel as though the target knee is the trigger to start the move back down to impact. Guess what? They are all right! Use whatever works for you.

Rhythm and Blues

Arthur Murray had it figured out when he taught millions of people with two left feet how to dance. He was able to turn what seemed to be awkward, mechanical movements into dancing with a simple sequence of 1-2-3, 1-2-3. Sheer genius!

Here is the cupped position at the top of the swing. There is no way you could hold a tray in this position—now that you have looked at it, wipe if from your mind!

That is what we are looking for in the golf swing—a rhythm and tempo that will take your mind off your thoughts and get you into the feel of the swing. The swing is not a rushed, forced, or mechanical motion. It is a like a dance.

Many golfers use metronomes to achieve a certain rhythm. Others just count, or use words that rhyme. Some even recite their names. Johnny Miller used to do this when he played on the PGA Tour. He would recite "Johnny" on the way up and "Miller" on the way down. So his tempo was John-ny . . . Mill-er. Of course, this is only good if you have a name like Nan-cy Lo-pez! I doubt Danielle Ammaccapane would be a candidate for this one! If your name doesn't work, feel free to use mine.

Once you find your own rhythm and your wrists are set at the top of your swing, the transition happens as your weight naturally shifts back to your target foot. Remember, you are a dancer at this point. Good rhythm can overcome a minefield of errors. But without good rhythm, you will definitely be swinging the blues!

Hip, Hip, Hurray!

Thanks to my friend and golf partner Dr. Frank Crinella, we know that women turn more with their hips than men do during the golf swing. Dr. Crinella has done extensive research on this portion of the swing, using both PGA and LPGA professionals. He has found that women turn their hips much more freely than men.

On the other hand, because men cannot achieve the same free turning action with their hips, it looks as if they are intentionally resisting their turn, when in fact they are only turning as much as their larger and less elastic muscles will allow. Their anatomy allows them to develop more resistance and generate greater power from their upper bodies.

This is why the "X-factor" theory of instruction is not ideal for women. It is based on restricting the hips on the backswing so the

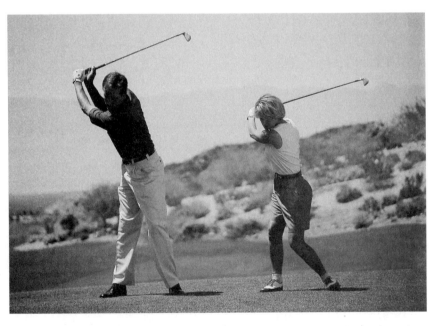

Men create extra power in the swing by coiling the upper body against the hips. A woman generates power by coiling her hips against the ground. We were built to swing this way—it's natural!

shoulders can turn against them as they coil away to create more torque (muscle tension), resulting in more power on the downswing. This may be great for men who are blessed with powerful upper bodies, but not so great for women who are not. Hip resistance in women golfers can be a disaster.

To achieve this X-factor position women must attempt something that is not natural—to resist turning the very hips that were built to turn. If you are one of the great number of women who have had instructors tell you not to turn your hips, forget it! Let it all hang out and swing with what God gave you. As Kelly said, "It's natural."

Your goal is to use your hips like a spring. They must coil against the ground, and the resistance comes from your rear knee and rear foot.

When you transition to the forward swing, let the hips loose. You may feel as though you are "spinning" as you return the clubhead back to impact. In reality, you are. That's fine.

In fact, if you look carefully at a picture of a man and woman at impact position, you will notice that a woman's hips are turned more open than a man's. This is because women are usually swinging on

75

Keep your target heel low to the ground while you turn your hips, coiling against the ground to add extra power and stability to your golf swing.

a flatter plane, and their hips are doing what they do naturally—turning.

Dr. Crinella also discovered during his extensive testing and research using Tour players that women are up on the rear toe sooner at impact than men. He pointed out that Laura Davies finished up on both toes at impact. I have noticed that I am up on my rear toe at impact, but I don't have the momentum or speed to come up on both toes. Dr. Crinella elaborated on this difference:

> Women, more than men, are generating a great deal of torque with their hips before impact. The male will generate some initial torque, but then the hips slow down after the clubhead achieves impact. Then, the hips begin to rotate again.
>
> Because women are generating all of this extra hip torque, there is a tendency for the lag of the club (whip of the shaft) to release early and chunk the ball on the way down behind the ball. All the more reason for women to get up on their back toes at impact. They need the elevation of the shoulders and arms, simply because their strong hips overpower their wrists and forearms.
>
> Getting up on the back toe momentarily for women slows the hip rotation, allowing the club to un-cock more fully, like the cracking of a whip. If the hips simply spun around in a circle at the same rate of speed, the clubhead would be out (outside of plane) and there would be absolutely no power.

According to Dr. Crinella, the correct impact sequence for a woman is:

1. Powerful hip rotation, causing you to spring up on the rear toe at impact, momentarily slowing the hips

2. Release of the angle (whip action created by shaft with clubhead), promoted by a momentary slowing of the hips

3. Continuation of hip rotation to avoid "throwing out" clubhead and finishing over the top to the inside of the swing path

My translation: Women turn their hips more than men, and so are more or less "spinning" when they return to impact. By springing up to the rear toe at impact, women slow down the spinning and elevate themselves, which helps to avoid hitting the ball fat and creates a whipping action that increases clubhead speed.

Impact

The photo below will show you some obvious differences between women and men at impact. Three points stand out:

1. My hips are turned more open than Brett's because they are spinning to my target side.

This photo illustrates three major differences between women and men at impact: a woman's hips are more open, she gets up on the right toe sooner than a man, and the right knee of a woman is turned inward and toward the target much sooner.

2. I am more up on my rear toe than Brett to slow the spinning of my hips at impact and create a "resistance" that acts similar to the resistance of cracking a whip.

3. My rear knee is turned in more than Brett's because my hips have spun open at impact. Brett's legs work more laterally, so his knees have more space between them.

Follow-Through

You may wonder why the follow-through is important if the ball has already been hit, but it is profoundly important if you want to hit the ball where you intend. If you want to hit the ball straight, it is important that the swing path of your golf club be swinging where you want the ball to go. I notice that my women students, more than the men, tend to swing back inside the target line as they follow through.

If you are pulling the ball, you are probably swinging immediately across the ball inside toward your body line after impact. This is a very common impulse. Body line is where your body is aimed; target line is the line created out away from your body where your golf club sets and aims.

This outside-to-inside swing path is often referred to as *over the top*, and it can wreak havoc with your game.

The tremendous centrifugal force and "spin" of a woman's hips is what creates the tendency to swing over the top from outside to inside of the target line on the follow-through.

Because what we feel and what we do may not always be the same, I suggest that you picture a clock face on the ground in front of you and imagine your target line bisecting the 12 o'clock position. On the downswing, return the clubhead down to 2 o'clock instead of 12 o'clock. Even though it may feel like the clubhead is swinging out to the right of your target line, you will most likely be swinging directly down the line. Have someone stand behind you to check your swing path and give you feedback. In time, you can change that 2 o'clock image to 12 o'clock and you will be back on target.

To correct pulling the ball, swing your clubhead out toward 2 o'clock until you acquire the feeling of swinging from the inside out. In time, you can change that 2 o'clock image back to 12 o'clock.

The 12 o'clock position is square to the target line—it just doesn't feel that way all the time.

If you have been swinging inside to 10 o'clock, which a lot of golf-ers do and don't feel, you are probably hooking or pulling the ball. By exaggerating your downswing inside to out so it feels as though you are swinging to a 2 o'clock position, you will most likely swing from an inside-to-outside path. I am compelled to say this one more time because I cannot say it enough: golf is a game that is played from the side, so feel it that way!

The Finishing Touch

"A balanced finish is the result of a good golf swing," my dear men-tor Johnny Revolta used to always tell me.

The finish position is important for anybody's golf swing, begin-ner or professional. Go to any tour event—PGA, LPGA, or Senior—and you will see pros practicing their finish positions all the time.

When I practice my downswing, I swing the clubhead directly through the ball and out toward the target in slow motion. Then I hold my finish position as if I am posing for the figure on the top of a trophy.

Sometimes it is just as effective to practice your finish position as it is to practice your backswing. That's because you have to do many things correctly in order to get the proper pose at the finish of your swing.

To practice your finish position, find a spot where you can see your shadow on the ground and check to see whether your finish is where you want it to be:

1. Target elbow is pointed down and angled at 90 degrees

2. Belt buckle is facing the target

3. Rear foot is up on the toe, weight on target side

Here is a good finish position as viewed from the back and side. Notice that my shadow tells me what my position looks like, so I can correct any errors.

This is a front view of the correct finish position. Pretend you are the statue on top of a trophy.

Graduation

Congratulations! You are finished with the full swing. I have talked about information overload as a theme throughout this book, and you have certainly been given a large dose of it.

I suggest you take your time and work on each part of the swing separately. When you are comfortable with each new change, move on to the next. Soon you will begin to experience the swing as a seamless whole, not a succession of parts.

If this chapter has thrown you into mental meltdown, I want you to take two aspirin and go back to lesson number one—impact. Forget about everything and hit the bag!

6

JOINING THE
DRILL TEAM

I never know who I am going to meet on my lesson tee. I just go to work and do what I do—teach. But some days, I get a big surprise!

This past season I met a woman named Marj Dusay who made me laugh the moment she arrived for her lesson. She is such a fun and lively character that we were attracting an audience.

I finally told Marj that she had missed her calling—she should have been an actress. Well, wouldn't you know it, she is an actress! Marj is Vanessa, the villainess on "All My Children." Of course, she is not that way in person, I assure you. She is hilarious, quick-witted, and smart. Marj lives in New York and was preparing to play in a celebrity golf tournament back home. She had only three days to get ready, so we did not have a lot of time.

To me, Marj represented a typical female because she was not interested in information at all. What she loved was the impact bag! Within minutes, she was blasting her 7-iron 130 yards down the middle of the driving range.

We decided we would work all three days and concentrate only on drills. This way, she would not take home a lot of technical information, and we could keep the lessons heavy on "feelings" and light on information. Marj liked this idea so much that she started singing the song "Feelings," and the whole range got into the act. We were really getting silly—a very womanly trait!

On the third day of Marj's lessons, many of the regulars who had seen her at the start of her transformation could not believe their eyes. She had taken her game to a new level, and she had made it look effortless. Marj called me from New York shortly afterward and told me she played superbly in the tournament and was still hooked. She wanted to know when I was coming to New York—not to see her show, but to play golf!

The idea of improving your golf game using drills is not a new one. But the idea of using just drills was perfect for Marj. Like many other women golfers, she wanted what worked, but she didn't want to have her mind cluttered with technicalities. She wanted to get the right feel because she knew she would be able to remember it later when she needed it. These are some of the drills Marj used during her lessons. I know they will work for you, too. By the way, Marj won the tournament!

84

Impact Drill

It would be a bit strange to carry an impact bag with you everywhere you go to play, so the next best thing is to simulate the feeling you get when you hit into the bag. Fortunately, this is very easy to do. Just find a steady object such as a tee marker, a tree, or even the back wheel of a cart. Press your clubhead up against it as though you are pressing into the bag. Look at your impact position and check it against the position you learned in Chapter 4. Correct any errors. In practicing the correct impact position, your goal is to get a sense of what it feels like to be squarely against the ball at impact. You can use the Impact Drill anywhere, any time to reinforce those good feelings.

I am practicing my impact position against the tire of a golf cart. The more you practice this position, the more aware you will become of what it feels like to be in good position at impact.

Swoosh Drill

This is a great drill to loosen up your swing and your muscles on the driving range. It also helps you to involve your hands and wrists in the swing. Grab your club right above the clubhead, rather than at the grip, and start swinging—pretend you have a baseball bat in your hands. When you hear the "swoosh" sound as you swing down, you know that your wrists worked correctly at the top of your swing.

85

Swoosh Drill. If the shaft of the club is not making a swoosh sound, then you are not swinging correctly or hard enough. Swing with speed and listen for the sound of power!

Preset Drill

If you have trouble getting your wrists hinged at the top of your swing, the Preset Drill is for you. To perform this drill, simply hinge your wrists at address before taking the club away—then perform your standard backswing. When you get to the top of your swing, your hands should be in the tray position, and you are ready to fire!

Feet Together Drill

Even the pros go back to this drill when they feel as though they are swinging out of control. By putting your feet almost together at address, your legs are silenced, and you are forced to swing within yourself instead of overswinging. Your attention is on the feeling of your upper body. Many players shut their eyes during this practice to enhance their feedback and balance. Once you get control of your upper-body motion again, slowly work your feet back out to your normal stance.

Preset Drill. In this drill, your wrists are hinged early at address. By starting with your wrists preset, you will acquire the "feeling" of being fully hinged at the top of the backswing.

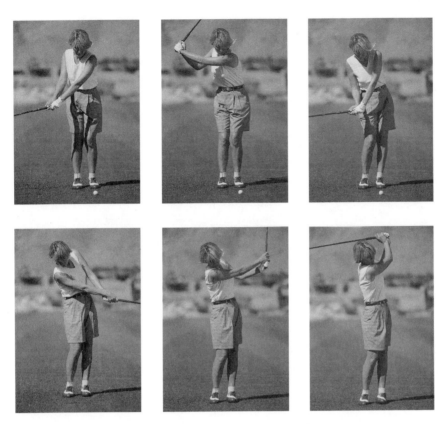

Feet Together Drill. This is a wonderful way to enhance balance. By keeping your feet close together throughout your swing, you are forced to stay in balance throughout. Notice how my arms and shoulders are forced to do the work because my lower body is fairly still.

87

Rear Arm Only Drill

This one is not easy, so tee the balls up before you attempt to hit them. Put your target hand in your pocket and take a short club, such as a 9-iron, and make three-quarter swings using only your rear arm. This will force you to fold your rear elbow on the backswing, then unfold as you swing back through to your finish. You will need a lot of strength in your rear arm for this drill, so grip down on the handle if you need to. Make sure you use a high-lofted club and follow through, facing the hole as you finish. Once you get the feeling

Rear Arm Only Drill. The purpose of this drill is to feel how your rear elbow folds on the backswing and unfolds on the downswing. Make sure you use a high-lofted club and only take a three-quarters swing in this drill.

of how your rear elbow folds and unfolds, you can add your other hand and continue to hit balls with this new awareness. If you can hit the ball solidly doing this, it will be a breeze when you add your other arm!

Target Arm Only Drill

In any good exercise routine, you can't work one side without working the other! You can get a better feeling of how the target arm operates during the golf swing with this drill. As with the previous drill, tee the balls up in advance, and put your "other" arm (in this case, the rear arm) in your pocket. Hold the club in your target arm and take a three-quarters swing with it. The club will feel very heavy and most likely be hard to control, so use your 9-iron and grip down on the club. Sweep the club back and away, keeping your arm fairly firm. Then, when you come through the ball at impact, notice how your arm swings out toward your target. When your arm gets about waist high, your elbow will naturally fold, much

Target Arm Only Drill. Notice that my target arm breaks slightly on the backswing, although I am trying to keep it fairly straight. Realistically, I can't keep it rigid while swinging so much weight with my weaker arm. But as I come back down and through the ball, the target arm does straighten out again. Notice the extension and hip turn through the ball, even with only one arm! It is only when I have extended on through to waist high that my target elbow relaxes and starts to fold.

like the rear elbow did in the previous drill. Remember, the target arm swings out and then folds. Register a feeling for this motion in your mind.

Chairwoman of the Board Drill

When I see a student struggling with her backswing, and she can't seem to grasp the feeling of keeping the clubhead low to the ground and extending the club away, I bring out my trusty two-by-four. You can get one at any hardware store. Place the board on the ground behind your golf ball. Execute your backswing by pushing the board backward with your clubhead. By keeping your clubhead low to the ground, you increase your extension and the arc of your swing for more distance.

Chairwoman of the Board Drill. I have to really push back with my target shoulder and arm to get that club started back. Now I am assured of a longer backswing with a bigger arc!

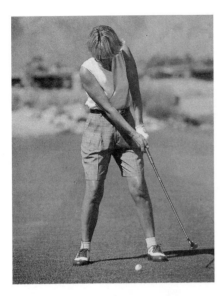

Clubhead in Front of Ball Drill. By starting in with the clubhead up and in front of the ball at address, it is much easier to sweep the clubhead away with momentum. Eventually, you will not need to do the drill at all. But if you ever freeze up again, you know what to do!

Clubhead in Front of Ball Drill

Sometimes a student seems frozen over the ball at address. She can't seem to swing the club away with any kind of rhythm. When I see this, I have her start her backswing at least 12 inches out in front of the golf ball toward the target. Of course, she must hold the club slightly off the ground and above the ball in order to do this. The long sweeping motion automatically creates momentum. This loosens the golfer up so that she eventually no longer needs a "jump start"— she has the rhythm.

Closed Stance Drill

This is a super drill to enhance the feeling of swinging from the side. Should you ever get into the habit of slicing your shots away from

Closed Stance Drill. Sometimes it is nice to exaggerate a motion so you can actually get a feel for it. By setting up in a severely closed stance position, with the rear foot dropped back behind the target foot, you are now insured of swinging from the more powerful inside to out swing plane. If you are having problems hitting the ball off to the right, this is the drill for you.

your body line, this is a wonderful way to correct that ball flight. Set up in an exaggerated closed stance, with the target foot far in front of the rear foot. This will help you swing the club away to the inside and back on through from the inside. Feel your hands intentionally turning over at impact, and deliberately hit a hook shot that curves across your body line. After you get the feeling for curving the ball again, by swinging from the inside, adjust your stance back to square and continue to swing on the more functional inside-out swing plane.

Through the Gate Drill. Don't get lazy with your practice. Set up two tees slightly wider than your clubhead. Focus on hitting directly through those tees and see just how solid you can hit the ball at the club face.

Through the Gate Drill

Often, your problem is not your golf swing; you are simply hitting the ball all over the club face. One way to improve consistency and tighten your focus is to put two tees together slightly wider than your club face and practice hitting balls between the two tees. You will get instant feedback telling you if you are swinging too far inside or outside at impact because your clubhead will hit either tee.

Swing into the Tree Drill

When I first started taking lessons from my mentor Johnny Revolta, he stuck two tees into the ground where he wanted my feet to be, then had me take practice swings toward some leaves on a tree. He told me not to stop swinging until I could hit one leaf, and then he left me. I could not believe I could possibly extend so far through the shot that I could hit any of the leaves. I stood there for half an hour, and still no leaves. Finally, he brought me some bandages for my hands and told me that was enough. We did this exercise a lot—some days I hit a leaf or two, some days I didn't. What I gained from it was one long follow-through with extra extension that has served me to this day. Find yourself a tree somewhere and see if you can stretch your follow-through just that extra bit.

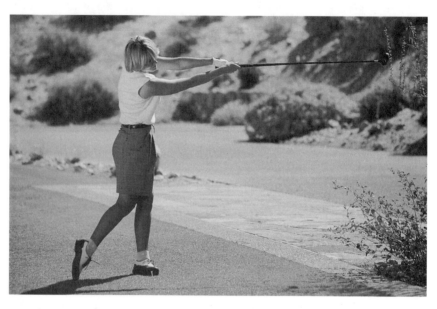

Swing into the Tree Drill. If you want to practice a longer follow-through, find yourself a tree with high branches and go to work!

PART III

FUNDAMENTALS
OF THE GAME

7

GOLF EQUIPMENT

Does Equipment Matter?

Yes—a great deal, in fact. Women most likely will need golf clubs with very different characteristics than men's. Your clubs may look like a man's, but they shouldn't play like them, unless that is how you play.

How Important Is Clubfitting?

Today we know clubfitting is important for good performance, so ideally you should get a set of clubs that are tailored for you. Hand-me-downs are no longer an option if you want to be serious about your game. If yours used to belong to your brother or dad or some other man in your family, you can take them to your local clubfitter to see if they can be salvaged. But eventually, you will want clubs that fit *you*.

Does Price Mean Anything?

Not necessarily. Certain equipment is made with metals that are costly or with an expensive manufacturing process. In clubheads, titanium is more expensive than steel because titanium is a more costly metal and is harder to manufacture. Graphite shafts are more expensive than steel because the production process is more complicated. A graphite shaft and a steel clubhead that feels good to you will work just fine, whatever the price. Titanium is more expensive, but it may not necessarily work the best for you. Test them out and see what works.

Are Oversized Clubs Better?

For most women—men too—a slightly oversized iron and an oversized metal wood give more confidence. But that does not mean these clubs are better. You still have to hit the ball with the center of the club face to get your best shot. That said, the larger heads are designed to improve your chance of hitting the ball on the club face. That's why so many people like them!

What to Look For in Golf Clubs

When you're shopping for clubs, you'll need to analyze many characteristics of each club. Following are some guidelines that might help you.

Shaft

Unless you are extremely strong, the best shaft type for all women will be graphite. The other option is steel, and you rarely see women using steel shafts today other than on the Tour. I changed over to graphite myself about ten years ago because it is so much lighter. Graphite enables many women to generate more clubhead speed than with a steel shaft, and this means more distance with each shot.

Flex

I am very big on a lighter flex shaft for women. I see far too many women working too hard to hit a golf ball. Again, I have switched to a lighter flex myself so I can swing with greater ease and let the clubhead do more of the work. The flexes are found on the shaft and are easy to see. Flex is how much bend the shaft will make during the swing; the lighter the flex, the more bend you can expect. More flex usually means more distance at the expense of control. A club fitter can help you find your ideal flex.

Club Length

Clubs need to be the proper length if you are to hit the ball consistently and solidly in the center of the club face. Unfortunately, many manufacturers seem to think all women are 5'4" and under. Many of the women's golf clubs today are too short for a lot of female golfers.

If one of my students encounters this problem, I order her a set of clubs that have a woman's shaft, but we add an extra inch so she is basically using a man's-length club. This allows her to assume a comfortable and natural address position when she sets up to the ball. Many manufacturers are aware of this and are already offering this service at no extra charge. Ask your pro or call the manufacturer and ask if they can do it.

Shafts: Brett uses steel, while I use graphite. Flex: I use a "senior" flex shaft, while Brett prefers clubs with a stiff flex shaft. Length: Brett and I would never be able to play golf with the same length golf clubs.

Offset refers to a club head that is set back away from the shaft. The club on the left has offset, while the club on the right does not.

Offset

Offset clubs have a face that is slightly set back from the shaft, a bit behind it. I like this design for women because it keeps the golfer's hands in front of the ball at address. It also promotes a higher ball flight for women with slower clubhead speed. Golfers who fight a slice ball flight will find that an offset club will also help to straighten that out.

Lie Angle

Lie angle has to do with how the sole portion of the club sets on the surface of the ground when you take your address position. Because we are all different heights and have various postures at address, not all clubs will fit each person.

If your club is resting on the heel portion of the clubhead, the club is too upright for you. From this lie angle you are likely to strike the ground with the heel of the club, causing the clubhead to close and the ball to cross over your body line in a hook-type ball flight.

If your club is resting on the toe portion of the clubhead, the club is too flat for you. From here, you will strike the ground with the toe, causing the club to open up at impact and sending the ball off in a direction away from your body line in a slice.

Either way, too upright or too flat, you are not making solid contact with the ball if the lie angle of your club does not set square against the ball at impact. I test my students all the time for lie angle with their golf clubs because I never want their clubs to be the excuse for crooked shots. Ask your pro to do the same. Next time you are buying a set of clubs, have them adjusted for lie angle before you walk out the door. This is becoming a standard practice at all good golf shops.

Loft

The *loft* of the club determines how high or low you will hit the ball. Lofts of clubs are measured in degrees; the higher the degree, the higher the ball will go. A woman's driver might have 10, 11, or 12 degrees of loft, while a lob wedge can have 60 degrees of loft. Every other club is someplace in between, and each has a purpose. Very rarely do I recommend that a woman's driver have a loft lower than 10 degrees, unless she is an extremely strong, advanced golfer. I also do not recommend women use longer irons (such as 3- or 4-irons) with very little loft. These clubs require extra clubhead speed to drive the ball higher into the air.

Grip

I am not as interested in what type of grip you choose as how that grip feels in your hands. A grip that is too large keeps the wrists from releasing at impact and results in a loss of distance with a push-type shot. A grip that is too small causes too much hand action, and often results in a shot pulled to the opposite direction.

Make sure you get fit for your grips so your fingers are almost touching when you wrap them around the handle. And keep those grips clean! It is not that tough to do—simply use soap and water.

If your grips are wearing out, get new ones. The grips are a very important part of your equipment, so you need to take care of them. Most people who play golf need new grips at least once a year. I get new ones at the start of every season.

Choosing a Set of Clubs

The selection of golf clubs is very personal. We all have different needs and preferences to consider. The first thing to do is ask your pro for advice when choosing irons—a typical starter set for women. I like a combination that includes a 5-iron up to a sand wedge.

Regarding woods, I advise my beginners to start out with a 3-wood through 7-wood. It takes a while to master the driver, so stick with the lighter, more lofted clubs that give you confidence. You could even get 9- or 11-woods. I love my driver, but I used a 3-wood when I started out. Whatever works is what you want.

Thanks to new technology, 3- and 4-irons are being used less and less by women, replaced by easier-to-hit, more lofted, fairway metal-wood clubs. Egos are not a factor for those who want to play better golf. Women welcome suggestions to better their games, even if that means teeing off with a 3-wood instead of the "typical" driver.

Brands

Major brands spend a lot of money on advertising, but don't let that fool you. Always try out the clubs you are considering buying before

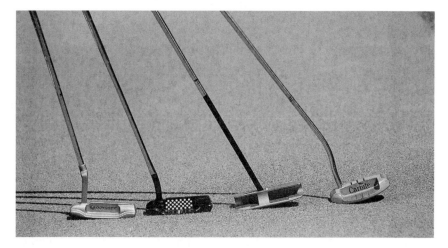

Putter selection is personal—take your pick.

you actually buy. In fact, take out a couple of different makes of clubs and hit with them one after the other to feel the difference.

This is what you are looking for when you do that:

1. **Trajectory.** Is the ball traveling high or low? Which do you like?

2. **Distance.** Does one hit much longer than the others?

3. **Feel.** How does this club feel to you? Do you like the feel of it better than the others?

4. **Sound.** Do you like the sound the club makes when it strikes the ball?

Putters

There are more styles of putters than there are flavors of ice cream, and putter selection is all about personal preference. Don't let anyone buy you a putter unless you try it out first. Most golf shops will let you practice putt with a new putter so you can test its feel. If you want, ask your pro for help fitting your style to a putter. The kind of putting stroke you have may mean you will do better with a certain style of putter. Some golfers stay with a certain putter their entire career, while others change putters every week. It's totally individual.

Do I Need a Sand Wedge?

Yes! The sand wedge was invented specifically to get the golf ball out of the sand, although you can use it for other shots too. The sole of a sand wedge is designed with a certain amount of "bounce," or big thickness of metal, on the sole. This extra thickness helps to bounce the clubhead into the sand and behind the ball to prevent the clubhead from digging too deep or going completely under the ball in deep grass.

Do I Need a Lob Wedge?

Lob wedges hit shots that go high in the air, land softly, and don't roll much. They have more loft than a sand wedge and less "bounce" on the sole. They are perfect for hitting over bunkers to the green. A lob wedge doesn't go very far. It may only go 20 to 30 yards, but if you play a golf course with a lot of deep bunkers or elevated greens, you may want to consider it. The key to being a good lob wedge player is to practice often, as it is very tough to gauge the distance the ball will travel with so much loft on the face of the clubhead.

Do Balls Matter?

Golf balls are sold with a variety of features, such as one piece, two piece, three piece, hard-cover, soft-cover, and so on. You even have a choice of compression, such as 80, 90, and 100. Supposedly the 80 compression is more suitable for women because it is designed for less clubhead speed. The lower compression golf ball is softer, so it will compress off the clubhead easier at a lower clubhead speed. I have yet to see a golf ball that makes any significant difference in any golfer's game. Sorry about that, I just haven't. I know women who use 90 and 100 compression balls and play wonderfully, and I know men who use an 80 compression ball and play great. Unless you hit the ball on the sweet spot the majority of the time, the golf ball will make almost no difference at all. Only the elite players can really tell a difference.

Select the brand of ball that gives you the most confidence. Test different balls out and choose for yourself. Don't let anyone influence you. You are the decision maker. Choose what *you* like.

Do I Need a Golf Glove?

Probably. A golf glove gives you a nonslippery contact with the golf club and can protect your hands somewhat from calluses. If you are right-handed, the golf glove goes on your left hand. If you are left-handed, the glove goes on your right hand. Some golfers will not use a glove at all. Those who do wear one may take it off when they putt because they get a better "feel." If that's the case, I say go for it!

Many years ago, while I was still dreaming about competing on the LPGA Tour, I worked at Mission Hills Country Club. Dinah Shore lived on the property part of the time, and she was a member. Dinah used to order her gloves two dozen at a time. She always wore a glove on *both* hands, so she would order a dozen rights and a dozen lefts. Years later I asked her why she did this, and her answer was typical Dinah: "Honey, I would never consider having an uneven tan line. If I am going to have one hand with a tan line, I must have two!"

8

ETIQUETTE, RULES, AND THE DEBBIE DOS

Etiquette Tips

Play Ready Golf

Make your decisions while you are approaching your ball or while you are waiting for someone else to play. It is not women in particular who play slowly—it is those who are not aware that they are falling behind the group ahead, or who just don't care. Whether you are male or female, slow play is rude.

Let Faster Players Play Through

This is an easy thing to do, and it will relieve so much stress to simply let the group behind you play through—both for them and for your group. If you are falling behind the group ahead and those behind you are waiting on you, do the right thing and let them through. You will be happy you did.

Take Care of the Golf Course

Fix your ball marks correctly, rake the bunkers, and replace your divots. This is standard procedure, and we expect this consideration from all golfers.

Be Aware of Others' Lines on the Green

Putting is a major part of the game. Many golfers take their putts seriously, so respect that. Be careful not to step on or close to another player's line on the green so she will have 100 percent of her attention on the task ahead, and so your footprints will not affect her putt.

Stand Outside Others' Vision

108

Certain people are very sensitive about seeing other golfers in their field of vision while they are playing a stroke. Respect their right to play a stroke without any distractions. Refrain from practice swings or practice putts that they may sense or see in their periphery.

Refrain from Talking While Someone Else Is Playing a Stroke

This is not an easy request for women—I know, because this is my own personal challenge! (I am not known as a walkie talkie for nothing!) Unless you are playing with your best friend, it is best to be aware of when a competitor is playing a stroke and keep your mouth shut. Even when you are playing a stroke, zip it and rip it!

Keep Track of Your Own Score

It is tough enough to play this game and deal with your own score, let alone trying to figure out the scores of others. Because golf is a game of honor, you are expected to keep track of your own score so that there will be no disputes or questions later. A good reputation can be easily destroyed over a simple game of golf, so be aware of how many strokes you take on each hole. Ultimately, your score is your responsibility.

Use Common Sense When Searching for a Lost Golf Ball

You are entitled to look for your golf ball for five minutes under the rules of golf. But if you are not playing in a tournament and the course is crowded, hit a provisional ball from the tee and do not spend too much time looking for a golf ball when people are waiting behind you for play to resume. Use common sense with this one; slow play is never a winning situation.

Be Aware of the Flagstick

If you are tending the flagstick and everybody agrees they do not need the flag, make sure you remove the flagstick in a proper manner without damaging the hole. Take the flagstick far enough away so that it is not in the line of vision of your playing partners. If you are the first to hole out your putt, you should be the one to get the flagstick and replace the flag when your partners have putted out.

Leave the Green When Everyone Has Putted Out

Move on to the next tee as soon as you are finished with each hole. Do not stand around discussing your score, and definitely do not sit in the cart in front of the green or off to the side figuring out how the match stands when other golfers are waiting to hit their shots up to the green. Once again, be aware of those behind you and the pace of play.

The Shadow Knows

Shadows are common in golf. They can be especially annoying on the putting green. Play heads-up golf and be aware that your shadow may be a distraction to your fellow competitor. Move to a position where your shadow is not an issue.

Tip the Help

Whether it is the car valet, the bag boys, or the locker room attendant, remember to tip the help when appropriate or in accordance with club policy. It is a reflection on females in general. We want all golf facilities to welcome women, so be aware and take care of those who take care of you.

Rules to Know Before You Go

The rules of golf are supposed to be simple, but they can become complicated. The complications come if you don't play by the rules because then you get penalty strokes. And nobody wants that. I can tell you from personal experience that nothing can destroy the fun and flow of a round of golf more than a rules infraction. Here are some basics.

Play the Ball Where It Lies

Unless you are on a sprinkler head or a cart path or out of bounds, except on the green, there is never an excuse to move your ball any other way except by hitting it with your golf club. A lot of people play *winter rules*, which means they move the ball around on the fairway to give themselves a better position to hit the ball on the grass—but this is a bad habit and is strictly against the rules in competition. If you never get into the habit of moving your golf ball, you won't ever have to worry about this rule.

Don't Touch the Sand in a Bunker or the Ground Inside a Hazard Line

It's a penalty if you do. You can rest your club on the grass outside the bunker or hazard. Just remember, don't ground your club or you will be grounded.

Avoid Fixing Spike Marks on a Green

You can fix marks left by balls hitting the green, but under the rules of golf, you can't fix spike marks. With the soft spikes golfers wear today, it is hoped that this will be a nonissue in time.

III

Hold your club above the sand before you hit a bunker shot.

No Asking or Offering Advice on What Club to Hit

Asking for or getting advice in competition gets you a penalty. The only person you can ask for advice is your caddie. Now, if you are learning, and you're out with your friends or having a playing lesson from your pro, that's different. But don't get into the habit of asking, "What did you hit?" before you hit your own shot. That's considered advice, and you'll be penalized. You *are* allowed to look into your competitor's bag and figure out what club is missing. If she has a club in her hand and you don't see a 5-iron in the bag, you know she hit a 5.

If It's Growing and Attached, Leave It Alone

Breaking, cutting, or bending branches or anything growing and attached, no matter where you are, is a penalty. If it's plant life, don't touch it. Play it where it lies. If you even look like you are destroying plant life to improve your swing, your competition will be all over you like crabgrass.

Refrain from Touching the Intended Putting Line

Touching the intended putting line is considered altering the line of the putt. It's a penalty. If you could touch the line, who is to stop you from making a track from the ball to the hole? That would be unfair to everyone.

You Are Responsible for Playing Your Own Ball

Put an identification mark on it. All you have to do is hit the wrong ball one time and you will never forget this rule again. The penalty is two strokes, so be creative and put your ID on the ball.

Know Your Limits

Take no more than fourteen clubs in your bag when playing in competition. This is the USGA (United States Golf Association) maximum, so count your clubs on the first tee. The pros do.

Tee Up Behind the Tee Markers

This one is easy to remember. You must tee up behind an imaginary line formed by the tee markers. You can use any area between the markers and up to two club lengths behind them. That's where you start each hole. I see this one broken all the time, so wake up and look like you know what you are doing.

Tee up behind the tee markers.

Lost Ball

If you lose your ball anywhere but in a hazard (and you see it land there), you must go back to where you hit your previous shot and hit another. Add one stroke to your score, and remember, you are allowed only five minutes to look for a lost ball.

The Waiting Game

If your ball is hanging on the lip of the hole, you are allowed a reasonable amount of time to reach the hole, and then you can wait up to ten seconds for the ball to drop into the hole. If it doesn't drop within ten seconds, you are required to tap it in.

Avoid Hitting the Flagstick on the Putting Green

Make sure you have someone tend the flagstick when you are on the putting green to remove the flag before your putt goes in the hole. If you accidentally hit the flagstick, you will be penalized two strokes in stroke play or loss of match in match play. Ouch!

The USGA Rules of Golf booklets are available at most golf shops for a modest price. They are small and portable—buy one and keep it in your bag so you'll have information handy. Your golf pro can explain a rules situation to you if you have a special question. If you can't find a USGA rule book, go to the USGA website (www. usga.org) to find out how to get one.

The Debbie Dos

1. Show up for your tee time with time to spare. Warm up, hit a few balls, make some practice putts. Then you will be relaxed and ready for a good round.

2. Hats and visors are good for blocking the sun, but if they are too big they can get in the way of your swing—or, worse yet, make you look like the Flying Nun.

3. Wear clothes that are loose enough for active movement. Golf is a game of physical motion. Whether you shop at a department store or pro shop, buy clothes that let you take a whack at the ball without ripping a seam.

4. Wear golf shoes. Sandals, flats, or heels (ridiculous as that sounds, it happens) will not give you the extra support and traction you need to hit a golf ball.

5. Wear light makeup. On warm days, heavy makeup melts.

6. If you can't get your nails into a golf glove, reach for the clippers or the file. Nails long enough to pass for lethal weapons won't help your score.

7. Wear jewelry that doesn't hit back. There's nothing worse than having a bracelet that gets in the way of your grip or a necklace that strangles you when you make a swing. Not to mention getting a bruise on your fingers from extra rings. Many women are able to play with their wedding rings, but if it hurts to hit the ball with the ring on, leave it at home when you play golf, or lock it in your car and put it back on after your round.

8. If you need to wear sunglasses, get a pair that has a good lens for golf. Many sunglasses distort your vision and make it impossible to judge distance. A Polaroid lens is always good for golf. Also, make sure the sunglasses are comfortable and will stay on when you hit the ball.

9. Check the dress codes when you play at a private club. Many have a nineteen-inch shorts rule. If you don't have proper clothes, you will not be allowed to play. Most private

clubs frown on revealing outfits. Save the low-cut tops for the beach.

10. Be prepared for emergencies such as the time of the month, headaches, allergy attacks, blisters, and so on. Pack a first-aid bag and put it in one of your golf bag zipper pockets. One of the best first-aid items is gauze tape (available at drugstores), which can be used on your fingers or thumbs to prevent blisters.

11. Wear sunscreen. Put it on before you go out to play, and pack it in your bag so you can reapply if necessary.

12. Have enough tees, balls, and ball markers for the entire round.

9

THE HANDICAP SYSTEM

Because *handicaps* allow people of differing skill levels to compete together, they have greatly contributed to golf's popularity today. Whether you play in individual events or team events, you will need a valid handicap to participate, so let's take a look at how the handicap system works.

The USGA is responsible for creating the rules and standards of golf play. These rules have never been known for simplicity, but the USGA has really hit confusion paydirt with handicaps! To add to the puzzlement, the handicap is sometimes referred to as a *handicap index*. Don't let the terminology throw you off—just remember that it's all handicap, period. Personally, handicaps drive me crazy. After competing on the LPGA Tour, there is nothing more annoying than giving strokes to an opponent. Nancy Lopez never gave me any strokes, so it has never been an easy adjustment for me.

Handicaps were devised because most golfers don't shoot par. A handicap is a percentage of the difference between your best scores and par. It isn't your average score. The USGA says that at least 75 percent of the time, your score minus your handicap won't equal par at your golf course.

If you want to get a handicap so you can play in events, ask your local professional for help. Or you may join a local golf association, and they will compute a handicap for you for a small fee. Before you can get an official handicap, you will need to record at least twenty rounds. From these twenty rounds, the ten lowest rounds will be used to make up your index.

If you are interested in the finer details of handicaps and want to know why women's and men's are different, go to the USGA website at www.usga.org. It has everything, including computation and formulas. You can learn more than you ever wanted to know!

Or you can skip the computing. All you have to do is record, or *post*, your score at your golf club, either on a handicap chart or into a computer, and let the magic of technology do the rest! Welcome to competitive golf!

The Course Rating

Every course is different, so the golf world has come up with a way to determine how to adjust the handicaps when you go from one course to another. The solution is the *course rating system*, and it has been a tremendous success.

A course rating is based on factors such as length, bunkering, width of fairways, difficulty of greens, water hazards, thickness of rough, out of bounds, and all kinds of variables that may make one course play harder than another. The ratings are done by members from state golf associations who play the golf course and assign values to it. The rating gives you an indication how closely the tees you choose to play compare to par on each hole.

The Course Slope

The *course slope* is often confused with the rating, but they are not the same. Every scorecard has a rating for each tee, such as front tees,

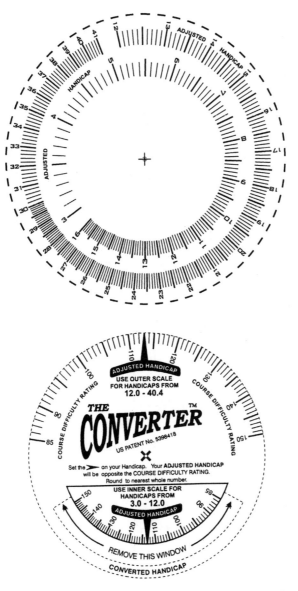

Handicap converter. To use the converter, first assemble the two pieces by carefully cutting out each wheel along the dotted lines, including the "window" on the smaller wheel. (Use the larger version printed at the end of the book.) Use a thumbtack or pin to line up the centers and hold the wheels together. Then set the large arrow on your handicap (12.0–40.4 are on the outer scale, and 3.0–12.0 are on the inner scale), locate the course difficulty rating on the same scale as the arrow, and read the number directly across from the course rating. Round off this number for the handicap you should use for this course and tee combination.

middle tees, senior tees, and so on. The slope rating measures all holes from the different set of tees and gives each course a number from 55 to 155. The slope rating helps to determine how many strokes you should get when you play a golf course away from your home course, or how many strokes you should get when you play a different set of tees. The more difficult the course or the farther back the tees, the higher the slope rating.

To give you an example of how confusing this can be, here's a scenario to consider. If your handicap is 25 and you play at a course with a slope of 110, this is what happens when you compete at a different course with a different slope rating:

- For a course with a slope of 125, you get three extra strokes.
- For a course with a slope of 100, you give your opponent two strokes.

I know from my own experience that most golfers don't care about how to determine handicaps, slopes, or whatever. All they really want to know is, how many strokes do I get for this particular course, from these particular tees?

OK. We have just made it easy. We are including in this book a handicap converter that you can punch out and put together yourself. My good friends Tom and Chrissy Jones from Phoenix have invented this little time-saver just for people like you and me. Put it in your golf bag and you can relax whenever a question regarding your handicap index comes up again.

The converter is a must if you play in competitions or travel to different golf courses. You will find yourself very popular on the first tee as you quickly compute each player's strokes for the day.

Competing Against Men: Get Your Strokes!

To me, one of the most interesting things about how the USGA computes the handicap for women is that they use a different system for the guys. Differences between men and women in length of tees and overall strength are figured in, causing a difference of anywhere from two to eight strokes, depending on where you are playing.

According to my friend Diane Williams, who is on the handicap committee of the Women's Southern California Golf Association, a woman who has a handicap of eight does not really play identically to a man with a handicap of eight. That's because the handicaps for men are calculated by taking into consideration the men's strengths and abilities from the men's tees, while the women's handicap is calculated by considering women's strengths and abilities from the women's tees.

Consider a scorecard. It may have separate ratings (and course slopes) for men and for women from the front two sets of tees. This makes it easier to figure out how many strokes you should get if you play the white tees instead of the red. However, not every course does this.

To give you an example of how the different course ratings can make a difference in how many strokes you get competing against a man, let's look at two typical scenarios from the USGA website:

1. Women on forward tees playing men from men's tees

If women playing from the forward tees where the women's course rating is 73.4, compete against men playing from the middle tees where the men's course rating is 70.9, the women will add 3 strokes (73.4 − 70.9 = 2.5 rounded to 3 strokes) to their course handicaps.

2. Men and women playing from the same set of tees

Since the women's course rating usually will be higher [than the men's tees], women receive additional strokes, equal to the rounded difference between the USGA Ratings, with .5 or greater rounded upward.

If women playing from the middle tees where the women's course rating is 77.3 compete against men playing from the middle tees where the course rating is 70.9, the women will add 6 strokes (77.3 − 70.9 = 6.4 rounded to 6 strokes) to their course handicaps.

According to the USGA, this always applies, so be sure you communicate this handicap trivia to all of your male friends when you figure the teams and competition for the day. Explain to them that the rating system is different for men and women, and that is why you get the extra strokes.

If I can ask for my strokes, and I am a pro, then I know you can do the same. All you are doing is leveling the playing field. Talk to your pro if you still have questions. Better yet, if you really want to get some answers, check the USGA website at www.usga.org.

10

ON COMPETITION

Competition is not and never has been an easy experience for me. It goes against my nature. I like to see everybody happy and living in harmony. The experience of competing throws me right into the "dark side," but instead of becoming Darth Vader, I become what I call the "Dragon Lady."

Competition is about winning and losing. It feels like war to me and I prepare for battle. My scales go up and my tail comes out the moment a bet is put on the table. My entire being and self-worth are on the line. Socializing goes out the window.

I wish I could say I am all alone when it comes to this type of reaction to competition, but I have seen a lot of bigger and meaner dragons, and I am not talking about certain pros on the LPGA Tour. Ask any women's golf league director how friendly women are in competition, and they will tell you to arm yourself!

The good news is that I am older and wiser now than in my Tour days. My fire has died down tremendously, so I have earned the right to lecture all my fellow dragons and would-be dragons about handling stress and staying focused during competition. Age does have its privileges.

What I know for certain is that everybody is as different in their mental attitudes toward competition as they are in their swings. What works for one person does not work for another. I am not going to play sports psychologist and tell you how you must think to be a good competitor. I am still researching that for myself! I am simply going to share with you some basics that will help you stay in control of your emotions in competition.

Drink Water

I will never forget a particular day last summer at the back of the Citrus Golf Range in La Quinta, California. Mike, one of my top college students from the San Diego State golf team, met Hollis Stacy, winner of three U.S. Opens, for the first time. I told him he could ask her anything at all about competitive golf, so he proceeded to ask her a most interesting question: "If you could share one thing about the secret to success in competition, what would that be?" I was very curious how Hollis would answer the question. She thought for a few moments, and then, looking him directly in the eye, unequivocally answered, "Water. Drink water."

That was it—Oz had spoken. Hollis went back to hitting golf balls.

Although I laughed out loud at the time, I asked her later what she meant by that. Hollis explained that during competition it is easy to get dehydrated from the stress. Many times she had found herself getting dizzy or fuzzy in her head as she was holding on for a win or charging for a comeback in competition.

Hollis has made it a point to remember to drink plenty of liquids during a competitive round of golf, especially toward the end. As it turned out, that was a profound tip after all! Drink fluids to be fluid!

Keep Your Chin Up!

A few years ago I participated in an enlightening workshop for teaching professionals taught by Fred Shoemaker of Extraordinary Golf. Fred did not focus on the golf swing, but on how a golfer's mind works. He explained that anyone can control being in the so-called *zone*, or what some players call *the present*. I was particularly interested in this topic because I have struggled with being in the moment while competing.

I used to get distracted by things that were out of my control, such as the idiosyncrasies of certain players I was paired with, slow play, or bad weather conditions. My ability to focus on the job at hand when I was a Tour player was poor, to say the least. Thank goodness I wasn't working with power tools!

Fred asked the group to walk for one full golf hole keeping chins up and eyes focused directly on the horizon. We were not to look up or down, just keep our eyes focused on the horizon for one full hole. This was my chance to do my Nancy Lopez imitation, as this is very much the way Nancy plays golf.

Of course, we were not allowed to talk for this exercise either, which almost put me over the edge—but I knew there was something to be learned here.

Within seconds I found that I let my gaze fall straight to the ground while I thought about what I had learned earlier in the day. I quickly looked up again and proceeded on. Seconds later, I looked up to the sky as I wondered what I would be having for lunch. I forced myself to look straight ahead again. This was a super-hard exercise for me, and I was failing miserably!

Finally, after what seemed to be an hour, we finished the exercise. Fred explained that when we look down, our minds are usually in the past somewhere—most likely dwelling on how we just blew a putt or missed a tee shot. When our eyes and head move up, we have probably moved into the future, anticipating what we need to do to bring our round back or how we can one-putt the rest of the way in.

When our heads are up and eyes are looking out in front of us, we are likely to be in the present, and that is where we want to be when we play golf. You can call this mental state anything you want, but it is when you are in the moment and are fully conscious of what you are doing at that given time. You are focused on the job at hand. Golf seems easy when you are in this state of mind.

No wonder Nancy Lopez looks so relaxed all the time! My advice is to practice this as often as possible. It may seem almost impossible at first, but you want to become aware of how you are holding your head during competition. Why play in the past or future when you can choose to be in the present? Keep your chin up!

Breathe

It might be hard for you to believe I would need to suggest breathing during a round of golf—obviously, you have been breathing, or you wouldn't be alive! But in a competition, when you can easily get stressed, it is very common for a person's breathing to become shallow and rapid. This causes the body to tighten up and not take in the oxygen needed to feed the brain and relax the muscles.

I have a little four-by-six card I put on my mirror at home that says "breathe," just to remind me to breathe in the midst of everyday stress. It would be a good idea to write "breathe" on your scorecard somewhere as a reminder.

It would be worth your while to explore different breathing exercises. Martial artists depend on breathing techniques in performing such feats as breaking stacks of bricks; golfers should be just as aware.

In competition, you are putting your focus on striking an object while your adrenaline is in overdrive, so prepare yourself for the challenge. We know that breathing reduces stress, so breathe!

Get in the Game

Competition can and should be a wonderful thing. It is the best way I know to sharpen your skills and get focused. Learning to overcome your fears and push through adversities is a growing experience. It builds strength of character.

The more you compete, the more comfortable you will become. You need to compete in order to know what happens to you under pressure conditions. Become aware of how far the ball goes when your adrenaline is flowing, or what happens to your putting stroke when you are standing over a three-foot putt for the win. There is a lot to learn about competition, and the only way to learn about it is to do it!

A Word of Advice from One Dragon to Another

Golf is supposed to be a self-governing game. If you want to make enemies quickly, start calling rulings on people. Don't get me wrong—I will be the first to call a ruling on someone when I feel that person has intentionally and knowingly cheated in a competition. It makes me sick, and it throws my game out of kilter, but it has to be done.

The key to a friendly competition is to try to avoid rulings altogether. If your playing partner or competitor forgets to move her ball marker back, tell her! If you see her about to make an illegal drop, tell her! If she is teeing off in front of the markers, tell her! You are only treating your fellow competitor the same way you would want to be treated.

You have a choice of how you want to behave in competition. You can either be a dragon or a respectful human being!

PART IV

ODDS AND ENDS

11

FIT TO HIT

People ask me all the time: What is different about playing on the LPGA Tour today compared to when I played in the late 70s and 80s? (Other than the money.) That's easy—the biggest change I see is that fitness has become an integral part of the sport.

This applies to all of the tours—the LPGA, the Senior, and the PGA. Everybody is getting into fitness—and if you are not, you are losing ground for sure. That is why all three supply a traveling fitness trailer to provide a convenient place to work out.

It is not unusual to see players hire personal fitness trainers. Nancy Lopez did this a few years back, and her results were tremendous.

When I was traveling on the Tour, I would attend aerobics classes with Jan Stephenson. Jan is one of the most disciplined athletes I have ever seen. When I watch her career and see how well she continues to compete today, I am not at all surprised at her success.

Jan has taken good care of her health and fitness in order to sharpen her competitive edge. And winning has been the name of the game for Jan Stephenson! She is in my opinion the pioneer of fitness for women on the LPGA Tour.

Let's Get Physical!

If you are serious about your golf, get serious about your fitness. I am not going to pretend I am an expert in this area because I am not. If anything, I was not very disciplined about fitness training when I was competing on Tour. We were not as aware of the advantages of strength training as the younger players are today.

What I do know is that golf is a game of feel, and the means of experiencing feel in your swing is your muscles. Because muscle movement is initiated in the brain, it makes sense that the better your muscles are trained, the better your brain will be able to memorize and repeat certain movements.

I am sure you have heard the term *muscle memory*, probably with reference to your golf swing. In order to help develop muscle memory in my students, I have them repeat a single swing motion until they feel as though it is automatic.

The bottom line is that a training program for flexibility, strength, and endurance is essential if you are serious about your golf game, and even more so after you pass the age of thirty. Thirty is the magic number where muscle structure supposedly starts to degenerate.

You need to start a fitness regimen, not only for your golf game, but to prevent injuries and to ensure a long, healthy life.

Strength Training

Power golf is the future of all professional golf tours. I remember when the game used to be a game of finesse, and the biggest stars were the best shotmakers. The game has changed dramatically due to the popularity of strength training.

Before you run out and buy weights or join a gym, it is very important that you consult with a professional trainer because strength training can be downright dangerous if the exercises are done incorrectly. In fact, overactivity in one body part can increase your risk of injury.

To maximize your effectiveness in your golf swing, you must use the entire body. This is especially so for women because we use our upper and lower bodies equally in our swing. We need a balanced strengthening program if we expect a balanced swing.

It is important that we strengthen everything—neck, shoulders, rotator cuffs, hips, abdomen, back, upper legs, lower legs, forearms, wrists, hands, and fingers. If you are anything like me, you are exhausted just hearing about it!

Endurance Training

It is not unusual for a golfer to tell me that she really had a good round going, only to run out of gas with just four or five holes to go. Once again, I plead guilty to this myself.

Poor cardiovascular endurance is not a good excuse for poor golf! This problem can be remedied by an aerobic exercise routine. Although golf is not considered to be an aerobic sport, carrying your own bag for eighteen holes can be a very good way to burn calories and get into better physical condition.

If you are allowed to carry a bag when you play, carry one with a double strap so you do not hurt your back while you are getting your exercise! From the forward tees, most golf courses are between 5,200 yards and 6,200 yards (or about 3 to 3½ miles) in length. Walking with your bag on your back for four or five hours means you can burn 700 to 800 calories!

Other ways to work on your endurance are not as much fun. At least you have many options to choose from so you can mix it up. Today, the most popular endurance exercise machines are the stairclimber, treadmill, stationary bike, and rowing machine. (Kind of makes that bag on your back look very appealing, doesn't it?)

A few years back I bought a very expensive stairclimber and put it directly across from the television so I could watch my favorite shows while working on my endurance. Unfortunately, after a while I did not use it very often. My husband claimed it was the most expensive clothes rack he had ever seen! Last month we gave it away to a good friend.

Flexibility

Patty Curtiss, an LPGA teaching professional and, in my opinion, a top fitness expert, tells me that women are indeed built with less muscle mass than men. While the disadvantage of this is that we have less strength than men, the advantage is that it gives us greater flexibility than men. Greater flexibility means that we are less prone to suffer pulled muscles than men. But if you don't stretch, you can't expect to stay flexible for very long!

Do yourself a big favor and look into exercise classes or a health club that stress stretching and flexibility training. Many of my friends are now taking Pilates classes (an exercise method that concentrates on building strength and flexibility, improving coordination, balance, and posture, and increasing stamina) and yoga classes just for the wonderful stretching rewards. Are these classes helping them with their golf games? You bet!

You want to stretch just prior to playing rather than an hour before you get to the course. By then you may have stiffened up all over again. Here is the routine I use before I even hit a golf ball. I work from the head down.

Neck

1. **Tilt Stretch.** Start out standing or sitting and slowly drop your head toward your right shoulder. Return to the center and drop your head to the opposite side. Hold for ten seconds on each side.

2. **Side Stretch.** Stand or sit and slowly turn your head to the right. Feel free to put your hand on your chin and apply more pressure for a good stretch. Return to the center and turn your head to the left. Hold for at least ten seconds on each side.

135

Tilt stretch

Side stretch

Arm and shoulder stretch

Arms and Shoulders

Stand or sit upright, flexing your abdominal muscles to support your back. Gently pull your right elbow across your chest toward the opposite shoulder. Hold this stretch for at least ten seconds. Return to the start position and repeat the exercise with your left arm. Keep your body facing forward.

Hips

Stand with your feet hip-width apart with your toes pointed out slightly. Keeping your knees slightly bent, place your left hand on your left hip for support. Extend your right arm up and over your head as you reach for the sky, so to speak. Slowly bend at your waist

Hip stretch

to the left without tilting forward. Remain tall. When you feel a good stretch, hold this position for ten seconds. Return to your start position and put your right hand on your right hip and extend your left arm up into the air. Slowly bend to the right until you feel a good stretch. Again, give it at least ten seconds. Not only is this a good stretch before you play, but if you catch yourself tightening up on the fairway, you can use it to keep your hips loose.

Lower Back and Upper Legs

Let your upper body fold and drop down in front of you. Your knees are bent and your arms hang down to the ground. If you can touch the grass, that is great—if not, no big deal. This is just a stretch, not a competition. After about ten seconds, shift your arms over to your right foot and hold again for ten seconds. Then shift to your left foot and do the same thing. Repeat this exercise as many times as you feel you need it.

Lower back and upper legs stretch

Standing quads stretch

Standing Quads Stretch

Sometimes I call this the Flamingo Stretch because I feel like a flamingo standing there on one leg. But this is a great stretch not only for your upper legs, but for your balance! Lift either leg and pull the heel of that leg close to your buttocks. Push your hips forward to tighten the stretch. Hold for ten seconds and switch legs. You can do this as many times as you feel necessary.

Hamstrings and Feet

The hamstrings need to be stretched and warmed up before any physical activity, including walking. Instinctively, we seem to know that, so we search for something to stretch against. Luckily, all you

Hamstring and foot stretch

need is a wall, a post, or a golf cart. When using a golf cart, lean forward and hold on to the sides of the cart. Pretend you are taking a gigantic walking step, but keep your back heel down, flat on the ground. Hold for about ten seconds, then switch legs. This will not only stretch out your hamstrings, but it will also stretch out your heels and feet.

Debbie's Personal Favorites

Here are a few tricks I've found helpful over the years.

The Grip Trick

You can do this exercise on your way to the golf course. I use a tennis ball, but you could also use one of the many hand grippers on the

Grip Trick   Rubber Band Trick

market. The object is to repeatedly close your fist using your hands and fingers closing in against the ball. This is a particularly good exercise for women because we do not have the natural hand and finger strength men do.

The Rubber Band Trick

Although the grip exercise is great for strengthening the hands and fingers, you would be doing yourself a disservice if you were to exercise your fingers in an inward motion only. A good exercise routine is one where you work your muscles in both directions. That is why I suggest you wrap a rubber band around your fingers and expand your fingers outwardly. This way, you will be working your fingers in the opposite direction. Although you will not lose any weight with this particular routine, at least you can tell your friends you have taken up "cross training"!

Warm Up with Intelligence

You always want to be cautious about injuries, so allow yourself time for an intelligent warm-up session on the range. This is the best way to avoid injury. Take your time and work your way up, starting with your shorter irons and moving up to your driver.

I personally start with my sand wedge, then alternate my clubs up to a 9-, 7-, 5-iron, 5-wood, 3-wood, and finally my driver. Too often, golfers are in a hurry to hit the longer clubs without being fully warmed up. All you have to do is pull a muscle one time, and you will be cured of that habit!

Simply the Best

The number-one exercise for any golfer who wants to develop greater strength for golf is to simply hit a lot of golf balls. You need to prac-

Warm up

Hit golf balls   Swing from the opposite side

143

tice actions needed for your sport in order to strengthen the muscles needed for that sport. It is not unusual for a rookie golf pro to gain 20 yards on her drive during her first year on Tour merely because she is hitting golf balls every day for a living.

I can always tell how committed a student is to improving her game by the amount of time she puts into hitting golf balls. It is amazing how quickly the human body will respond to repetition. Golf is fabulous that way.

The key to hitting a lot of balls at a single session is to remember that we must exercise with balance. Golf is played totally from one side, so it is very stressful on the lower back. To counter this excessive twisting of the lower back muscles, turn around at the end of your practice and take a few practice swings from the opposite side. Don't worry about your form—you just need to counterstretch those muscles just as you would when working out at the gym.

No wonder so many golfers have back problems! Take care of that back and it will take care of you!

Walking (especially nice on the beach in Huatulco, Mexico)

Walking

As Shivas Irons once said in the classic golf book *Golf in the King-dom*, "It's all in the walkin'." Yes it is, and that is what I personally miss most about playing on the LPGA Tour. I miss the "walkin'" with my caddie by my side and my putter in my hand. I will always walk when given the opportunity because it is the safest, most relax-ing exercise I can think of. Sometimes I carry two small weights to work my arms and shoulders while I am walking.

Happiness, for me, is very similar to what Shivas Irons said, but in three parts: "the walkin', the golfin', and the talkin'!"

12

MIXING BUSINESS
AND GOLF

One of my closest friends and business advisors is a woman named Susan Pappas from Connecticut. I met Susan years ago when I was the spokesperson for a women's golf event and she was both a consultant and contestant.

It didn't take long for me to recognize that Susan had her act together. I watched her take control of business and get things done. I have always admired women who were successful in business because that is something I always wanted to do myself. Until this golf tournament, the only business I had ever contemplated was "monkey business." I knew I could learn something from this woman, so I watched her with interest.

Everyone jumped into action when Susan spoke, and she was quick to delegate and organize her staff. I wanted to find out how she became so successful that she could own her own marketing communications business.

After the last day of the tournament, I asked her about her career and how she had accomplished so much at such a young age. (She was not even forty years old yet!) Susan shared with me that her secrets were to work extremely hard, and to use golf for relaxation and enjoyment away from the office, and for business as well.

Any woman who is serious about getting ahead in business needs to incorporate golf into her strategy for success. Some of the most successful male CEOs in the country have. Men such as Jack Welch of General Electric, Charles Schwab, and Donald Trump use golf to further their business relationships.

Even the dot-coms are using golf today. Bill Gates has become an avid golfer, and Scott McNeely of Sun MicroSystems has added golf to his success strategy. If these nabobs of the old and new economies are utilizing golf in their business strategies, why shouldn't women? Women can use golf to get ahead in the companies they work for and network with others outside of their work to get more business. Despite these obvious business advantages, women often say they do not have the time to learn golf. The real question I would like to ask is, "Can you afford *not* to play golf?"

Not only is golf a business tool, but consider this: a golfer shares the following qualities with successful business people. They both:

- Face suddenly changing conditions that require quick decisions
- Need to process large amounts of information to make a decision
- Require practice and preparation for a good performance
- Must perform under pressure
- Rely on a positive attitude

The strategies used in golf apply to individual business performance and success. What better reason to play golf?

Aside from what golf can teach you that you can put into practice in your career, golf provides you with an opportunity to spend time with people and get to know them. Where else but during a round of golf would you have four or five hours of essentially uninterrupted time to talk to someone and learn about his or her likes, dislikes, and philosophy on business and life? Not when you are playing tennis, hoops, or racquetball.

Golf allows you to build personal relationships with the boss, potential clients, suppliers, and others. Influential or important people who are usually rushed or difficult to talk to during the day can be won over easily during a round of golf.

The game also gives you insight into the other person's inner self. Watching how people conduct themselves while playing golf, which is above all a game of honor, will give you insight into each person's decision-making abilities, integrity, temperament, and sense of humor.

An important note: rarely is business discussed during the round itself. Business is saved for the 19th hole, which is the bar or grill in the clubhouse, or at a later date to be decided between parties.

We can all choose to do business with anybody—it just so happens that most people will choose someone they know, trust, and like. Often, this is what comes out of a simple round of golf.

Susan Pappas is no dummy—her business has grown even larger than when we first met years ago. If you are serious about your business, I suggest you look into how you can grow it through golf.

If you are very new to the game and want to learn more about how to mix business and golf, one way to get help is to call the Executive Women's Golf Association (EWGA). Today there are ninety-three EWGA chapters spread across the country. They conduct clinics for newcomers that cover the rules of golf and hold events, which are a great way to break in and to meet other women executives who like to play golf. The EWGA website is www.ewga.com, and they have a toll-free number: (800) 407-1477. Good luck!

13

DIVORCE COURSE

I love my husband, John, and I am very aware that he is a problem
solver. It comes in handy in his work, and it certainly doesn't hurt
when I need help solving one of the countless problems I am always
getting into. It's just that I don't want him solving any problems
with my golf swing. If I need my swing fixed, I will see a pro.

Husbands should know better than to offer driving advice to the
ones they love, either on the highway or on the fairway.

Let's put this in perspective: A surgeon would not perform an
operation on a family member in the hospital, nor would a lawyer
represent a spouse in court. Yet many husbands become instant golf
pros when their wives or children hit balls or play golf. They can't
seem to help themselves!

Many of these well-meaning spouses have done extensive research
on golf theories while on their own quest for the perfect swing.
They have read all the magazines, watched The Golf Channel, and
purchased every instructional video ever made. They are equipped
with the latest and greatest information the game has to offer, and
they know just who needs it: the wife, the kids, the aunt, the grandmother, and the dog!

Now, I happen to believe most men are sincerely trying to help when they explain to their loved ones how to play golf. Unfortunately, the very idea that something needs to be "fixed" implies to most women and children that they are not OK, that something must be wrong with them. Of course they are going to get upset. Anybody would!

Men are no different. Imagine if the roles were switched! Author and communications guru John Gray recommends that a woman never give unsolicited advice to a male. He usually interprets this as critical and unloving, and considers it offensive. But men tend to do to their loved ones the very thing that is offensive to them. This is a real dilemma.

One couple I work with, Stan and Sandy, laugh about this all the time because they are so aware of it. Stan wants advice on how he can contain himself, while Sandy wants advice on how she can communicate to him to get him to stop giving advice.

The very fact that they are aware of the tendencies is a good start. Don't let this ruin your relationship! Talk about it. Make light of it, and understand that guys are being guys. They cannot contain themselves—fixing is what they do!

If you are a beginner and your husband or significant other plays golf, the best thing you can do for your relationship, whether he is a beginner or just won the state amateur, is to make a few deals that you both can live by. I know many people in successful relationships who have done this very thing, including John and me.

1. **Acknowledge the problem.** Realize—both of you—that this is a difficult situation, and make a concerted effort not to ask, offer, or suggest anything instructional during a round of golf.

2. **Admit you know he's trying to help and that you appreciate it, but affirm that it does not work and makes things worse.** Tell him you want to get your lessons from a teaching pro who understands your game and what you are trying to do. Be nice about it.

3. **If necessary, draw up a written contract.** Men seem to understand and appreciate deals made in writing. Promise that you will not give him any lessons if he promises not to give lessons to you. The very thought of your telling him what to do with his golf swing will be enough to make him shudder.

4. **When playing couples golf, split up the couples.** That way you can't be coached in the cart on the way to and from every shot. Everyone can play his or her own game. Tell the guys it will speed up play if the women go to their tees together, because it will.

Golf is supposed to be a fun game—keep it that way!

As my good friend Dr. Maxann Shwartz, LPGA teaching pro and psychologist, advises, "The best way to help a spouse improve his or her golf game is to not fix what is wrong. Simply give support, encouragement, empathy (for bad shots), praise (for good shots), and love—lots of love! What most people are looking for in golf as well as in life is unconditional acceptance, regardless of their imperfections." It is endlessly sought, seldom found, so easy to give!

Women, ask for that kind of acceptance from your spouse or loved one. Show him this chapter if he has a bad case of the fix-its. If he still doesn't get it, then perhaps you had better see the Honorable Judge Judy. She will explain the situation to him in plain English, something like "STOP IT!"

14

SEX, LIES, AND VIDEO APES

The use of digital cameras and computers for instruction is hot, hot, hot. Videos don't lie. They give instant feedback of what is. The biggest reason video instruction is so popular today is that men love it, and men drive the market. They love to explore what is wrong with their swings, and they want to start fixing ASAP. The use of computers and video is a problem solver's delight.

Visual feedback can be a valuable tool for learning the game of golf, if it is used correctly. If not, this technology can mess up your head faster than you can say *fore*. With too much video feedback, you can easily get lost in the zone—the "Twilight Zone"!

Knowing what you do wrong does not tell you how to do it right. This past season at The Reserve we were able to put a computerized video system on the driving range. It got plenty of use—by approximately 90 percent of the male members. The use ratio was about 10 to 1 favoring the guys. During one full season, I gave just one lesson to a female student using the new computer system.

The most common response from my women students when asked whether they wanted to watch their swings on the video monitor was "Not today—I don't look good today."

This does not surprise me. Thanks to the research done by my friend Dr. Bruce Ogilvie using women athletes from various sports, we know that women internalize negative feedback more than men. That explains why women are not so excited about video. There is a lot of negative feedback to digest after a close-up view of your golf swing, especially when the pro starts putting up all the lines and circles highlighting what is wrong and where you are supposed to be.

It can really get comical at times. One of the funniest moments of our Disney Golf School for Women was when Hollis Stacy decided she wanted to give video lessons. I wondered why all the women were laughing so hard at her station. Then I discovered Hollis was adding her own doodles to the screen, such as tails, glasses, funny hats, and big hair. Hollis was even throwing in instant video liposuction for free! So much for the video lessons!

I do recognize the value of video; it can help a teacher talk about and demonstrate swing positions that are hard to describe. It is also extremely helpful for the more advanced golfer, who might be doing something so slight that it is hard to pick out with the human eye.

The advantage of video is that what you see may not match what you feel. Everybody's perception is biased by feel. What you feel to be a flat swing may in fact be an upright swing. Video can prove to be a powerful reality check.

Because I know computer analyzers and videos are here to stay, and because a lot of you will have an experience of learning by using a video, I have asked my Australian friend and fellow LPGA Tour player Penny Pulz to share some of her ideas about learning with video.

Penny is now the master of video lessons in Phoenix, Arizona. We recently worked together at a charity golf event, and I had Penny give me a lesson using her video equipment. It was such an outstanding lesson that I asked her for some "Penny Pointers" on taking video golf lessons. Here you go:

Dress Code

- Wear light colors—no busy designs on clothing.
- Headwear, caps, or visors are great for reference.
- Don't wear baggy clothing for video. We need to see what your body is doing.

When to Have a Video Lesson

- **When you are struggling with your golf swing and you want to see the shape of your swing.** You will get instant visual feedback with each swing, so you can make the changes necessary until you get the swing shape you like. What you see may not be what you have been feeling. You are matching what you feel to what you perceive to be the problem. Sometimes it matches, and sometimes it does not.
- **When specific areas of your swing are going haywire.** Areas such as footwork, hip rotation, grip, posture, and distance from the ball can all be observed closely with a video. The key is to take a close-up of that one particular area, so you don't bring in information that is not relevant to what you are working on at the moment. The focus of the lesson should not be on the video monitor, but on your swing as you are making the changes.
- **When you like the feeling of your swing and you are playing well.** This is the time to videotape at least fifteen minutes of your swing and play it in slow motion and stop frame positions. This will show you how your best swing looks. Imprint this vision in your brain. Take this tape home with you and play it as often as you can. There's nothing like positive reinforcement to improve your swing and your game.

When Not to Have a Video Lesson

The worst time to have a video lesson is just before you go out for a game of golf. When you are on the range, you are in your learning mode. Your brain is processing information and matching it to what you feel. On the golf course, you should be in your performance mode, dealing with targets and course management.

Beginners beware. Video lessons before a tournament can be disastrous to your game and mental heath! Advanced players, proceed with caution. Too much information leads to mental clutter. Keep it as simple as one swing thought.

Both Penny and I agree very strongly that video is just a tool to enhance a lesson by giving you feedback so that you can acquire the feeling that you are looking for. Golf is a motor skill. Your primary learning sense is kinesthetic. We both want you to "stay in touch with your feelings."

15

DEBBIE'S PICK
SIX TIPS

After all the research and the teaching I have done, if I had to pick six tips that would make the biggest improvement for most women golfers, these would be the ones. They are geared especially to women's bodies and women's needs.

1. Practice Correct Impact Position

Golf is a game of *feel*. Practice swinging into an impact bag, laundry bag, or old tire, keeping the clubhead square at impact. Focus on your arms swinging into the bag from the side, not over the top. Get used to the feeling of your head being behind the ball at impact. Take notice of how your rear knee and hips start thrusting forward for power. Feel how you come up on your rear toe. Reinforce this feeling on the golf course by setting your clubhead up against a pole, a rock, even the back tire of a golf cart, and push forward to emulate the feeling of impact.

You can practice the feeling of impact anywhere. Use the impact bag, or use whatever's handy, like the tire of your golf cart. Just reinforce that feeling of being square at impact!

2. Maintain Hip-Width Stance

It is an old belief that the stance is supposed to be shoulder-width for both men and women. We now know that for many women the stance needs to be at least hip width, especially with the driver. Hip width or even wider will provide greater stability and allow for a greater weight shift, which translates into more power.

Stance should always be at least hip width. A good stance gives you a strong and sturdy base to swing from.

Because your shoulders tilt at address, your eyes and head will naturally set up slightly behind the ball. This position will feel comfortable in no time, plus it makes it that much easier to transfer your weight back into the ball on the downswing.

3. Keep Your Eyes on the Back of the Ball at Address

At address, remember to position your eyes slightly behind the ball. From this position you are looking more at the back side of the ball rather than directly at the top. This will give you a sense of swinging sidearm and allow you to step forward on the follow-through just as a baseball or tennis player steps forward with the swinging motion.

4. Keep Your Arms Away from Your Body at Address

Contrary to what many of us have been taught—that the arms should hang directly down under the shoulders at address—the arms should come out slightly away from the body, depending on how tall you are and how much your body is bent over at address. Most women should set up to a driver with their arms reaching out far enough away from their bodies that the hands are at least under the chin at address.

Your height and setup position will determine how far away your hands will be from your body at address. You can see from my own setup that my hands are out past my chin. Most of the women on the LPGA Tour set up with their hands directly under their chins.

5. Your Target Arm Is a Tree Limb

Imagine your target arm is a tree limb, firm but flexible. It is straight, but not stiff. With your target arm working as a tree limb, you are certain to swing with a bigger arc and maximum control of your golf club. If it has a little give, that's OK—so does a tree limb.

Keep your target arm firm enough that your hands and wrists hinge at the top, but not so rigid that you lose power.

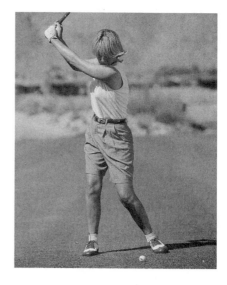

6. Let Your Hips Turn—It's Natural

You were not built with wider, more flexible hips than men for no reason. Use them in your golf swing! Turn your hips freely on the backswing, avoiding shifting your weight to the outside of your back knee or rear foot. Feel your feet rooted firmly into the ground. From this powerful, coiled position, you are ready to seriously thrust forward with your legs and hips as you uncoil to impact position. Continue to let your hips turn all the way open to your left side. All you have to do now is hold your finish and smile!

Give yourself permission to swing the way you were built to swing—using your hips! You can see from these photos that my hips turn a lot and I am swinging around my center the entire time.

AFTERWORD

Women and men are different, but that doesn't mean we can't enjoy this wonderful game equally and with each other. Our differences only serve to make golf more interesting. If we can laugh at our differences and understand each other better, we are well on our way to a lifetime of golfing enjoyment.

Personally, I believe that golf is something of a religion of its own. Many players get seriously worked up when it comes to their beliefs about the golf swing and how it works. There are plenty of books, magazines, and videos supplying us with various interpretations on how this so-called "game" should be played.

We can all debate the wrongs and rights of the golf swing, but it serves no purpose. The simple truth is that the right way is the way that works for you, period. There is no perfect swing, and there is certainly no golf prophet with all of the answers.

It doesn't matter if you get your information from your great-great grandmother, or from The Golf Channel. What matters is that it works for you and you enjoy the game.

My goal for this book was to share enough information, suggestions, and tips to inspire you to look at your own game. If this book has made just one change in your game for the better, I am thrilled.

It is often said we teach best what we most need to learn, so I am looking forward to using this material for my own improvement. I want to thank you for this learning opportunity. It's time for this particular Venus to take to the fairways and practice what I preach.

INDEX

Page numbers in italics refer to photographs or illustrations.

165

DEBBIE'S DISCOUNTS

Mention Debbie Steinbach to receive a 10% discount on these fine products:

Impact Bag
Golf Around the World
1-800-824-4279

Handicap Converter
Tom Jones
602-943-5104

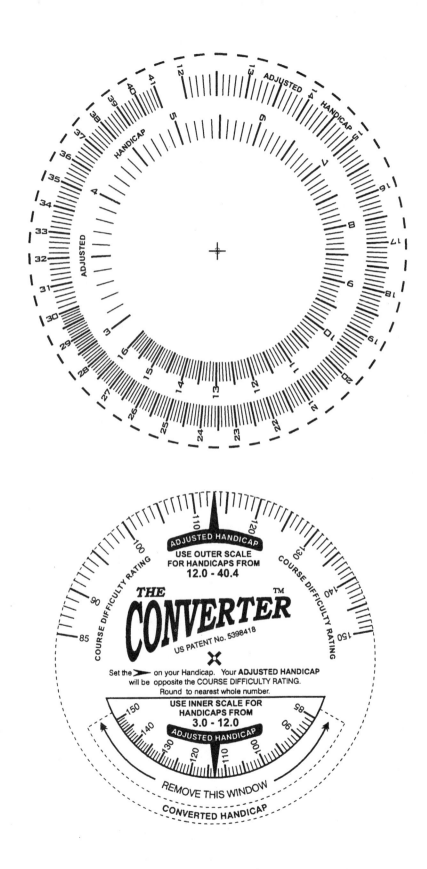

1-2-02

Lucia's Tips-
Swing
✓ Reach for ball

✓ "Impact" - left hand square to
target (release)(Toe of club into bag)

✓ "Impact" - rt knee towards target
(step into it!)

Chipping -

relax elbows - swing the "U"
pretend basketball between elbows

You Are Transformed!